WEHMAN'S BARTENDERS GUIDE

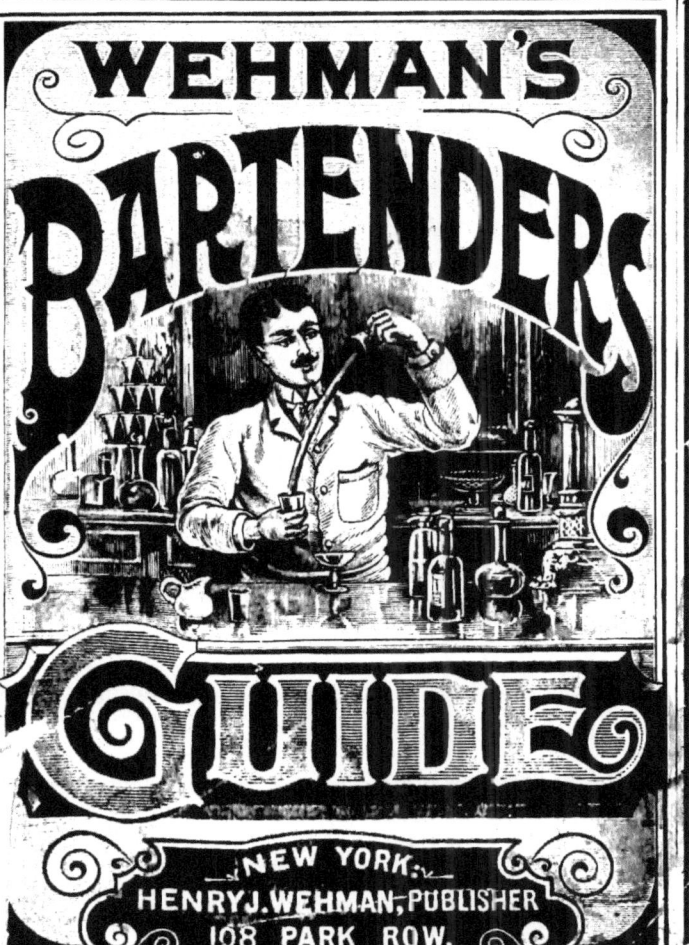

NEW YORK:
HENRY J. WEHMAN, PUBLISHER
108 PARK ROW.

WEHMAN'S

Bartenders' Guide,

—OR—

THE ART OF PREPARING ALL KINDS

—OF—

Plain and Fancy Drinks

BOTH

NATIVE AND FOREIGN.

A COMPLETE AND RELIABLE REFERENCE FOR HOTELS, SALOONS AND FAMILIES.

NEW YORK:

HENRY J. WEHMAN,

FACSIMILE EDITION
©2023 Moulin & Parole
www.moulinparole.com
ISBN: 978-1-958604-09-0

PREFACE.

TO those who cater to the patrons of Bars and Wine Rooms, as well as the varied tastes of the home circle, we dedicate this book. Within its pages will be found an infinite variety to gladden the soul, warm the heart, relieve life of much of its toilsomeness, and engender a spirit of fraternity and good feeling, which is commendable in all. Beverages of every nation and clime are here set down, wherewith even the most fastidious may have their appetite appeased, and any and every caterer can find something to please all applicants.

CONTENTS.

WEHMAN'S
BARTENDERS' GUIDE.

Absinthe—how to mix.—*(Use an Absinthe glass.)*

In preparing the above drink be particular and inquire whether the customer desires it in the old French style or on the new improved plan. Mix as follows in a large bar or Absinthe glass : 1 pony glass of Absinthe, place this into the large glass, take the top part of the Absinthe glass, which has the shape of a bowl, with a small round hole in the bottom, fill this with fine shaved ice and water ; then raise the bowl up high, and let the water run or drip into the glass containing the Absinthe ; the color of the Absinthe will show when to stop ; then pour into the large glass and serve. None but genuine Absinthe should be used, which you can easily tell by the color in mixing, as it will turn to a milk color and look cloudy, which the domestic article does not. This is what they call an old style French Absinthe.

Absinthe—American style of mixing.—*(Use a large beer glass.)*

⅜ glassful of fine ice.
6 or 7 dashes of gum syrup.
1 pony glass of Absinthe.
2 wine glasses water.

Then shake the ingredients, until the outside of the shaker is covered with ice ; then strain it into a large bar glass and serve. As this is mixed it is more pleasant to drink than the French style. The Americans are not in the habit of drinking Absinthe like the French, but a drink of it occasionally will hurt nobody.

This is called the American or frozen Absinthe.

Champagne Cocktails.—*(Use a Champagne goblet.)*

In mixing all cocktails, fill the mixing tumbler with fine shaved or broken ice, before putting in the ingredients. For a Champagne Cocktail it is best to place two or three lumps of clear ice at the bottom of the glass and then mix as follows: a small bottle answering for three, and a large or quart bottle for six:

2 or 3 small lumps of ice.
2 or 2 slices of Orange on top of the ice.
2 or 3 Strawberries.
1 slice of Pineapple.
1 lump of Loaf Sugar.
2 or 3 dashes of Bitters (Baker's or Angostura).

Fill the goblet with Wine, stir well with a spoon, twist a piece of Lemon peel on top, and serve.

In all cases where Fruits or Sugar are necessarily used, they should be handled with tong and fork. Decency demands this at your home table, and properly obtains over every bar to every applicant.

Martini Cocktail.—*(Use a large bar glass.)*

Fill the glass with ice.
2 or 3 dashes of Gum Syrup.
2 or 3 dashes of Bitters.
1 dash of Curacoa.
½ wine glassful of old Tom Gin.
½ wine glassful of Vermouth.

Stir well with a spoon, strain into a cocktail glass, squeeze a piece of lemon peel on top, and serve.

Manhattan Cocktail.—*(Use a large bar glass.)*

Fill the glass up with ice.
2 or 3 dashes of Gum Syrup.
1 or 2 dashes of Bitters.
1 dash of Curacoa (or Absinthe if required).
½ wine glass of Whiskey.
½ wine glass of Vermouth.

Stir up well, strain into a fancy cocktail glass, squeeze a piece of lemon peel on the top, and serve.

Absinthe Cocktail.—*(Use a large bar glass.)*

Fill tumbler with ice.
3 or 4 dashes Gum Syrup.
1 dash Angostura Bitters.
1 dash Anisette.
¼ wine glass water.
¾   "   "   Absinthe.

Stir well, strain into a fancy cocktail glass. Twist a piece of lemon peel on top, serve.

Brandy Cocktail (Fancy).—*(Use a large bar glass.)*

¾ glass filled with shaved ice.
2 or 3 dashes of Gum Syrup.
1 or 2 dashes of Bitters.
1 or 2 dashes of Curaçoa, or Absinthe if required.
1 glass of French Brandy.

Stir well with a spoon, strain into a fancy cocktail glass and squirt a little champagne into it, twist a piece of lemon peel on top, and serve. The champagne will only be added where it is kept on draught.

Vermouth Cocktail.—*(Use a large beer glass.)*

¾ glass of shaved ice.
4 or 5 dashes of Gum.
2 or 3 dashes of Bitters.
1 wine glass Vermouth.
2 dashes of Maraschino.

Stir up well with a spoon, strain it into a cocktail glass, twist a piece of lemon peel on top, and serve.

East India Cocktail.—*(Use a large bar glass.)*

Fill the glass with shaved ice.
1 tea-spoonful of Curacoa (red).
1 tea-spoonful of Pineapple Syrup.
2 or 3 dashes of Bitters.
2 dashes of Maraschino.
1 wine glassful of Brandy.

Stir up with a spoon, strain into a cocktail glass, twist a piece of lemon peel on top, and serve.

Soda Cocktail.—*(Use a large bar glass.)*

4 or 5 lumps of broken ice.
5 or 6 dashes of Bitters.
1 or 2 slices of Orange.

Fill up the glass with Lemon soda water, and place a tea-spoon filled with Sugar on top of the glass for the customer to put it in himself.

Do not let the foam of the soda spread over the glass in mixing the drink.

Whiskey Cocktail.—*(Use a large bar glass.)*

¾ glass of fine shaved ice.
2 or 3 dashes of Gum Syrup.
1½ or 2 dashes of Bitters.
1 or 2 dashes of Curacoa.
1 wine glass of Whiskey.

Stir up well with a spoon and strain it into a cocktail glass and squeeze a piece of lemon peel on top, and serve.

This drink is one of the most popular American drinks in existence.

Jersey Cocktail.—*(Use a large bar glass.)*

½ table-spoonful of sugar.
3 or 4 lumps of broken ice.
3 or 4 dashes of Bitters.
1 wine glass of good Cider.

Mix well and strain into a cocktail glass, and twist a piece of lemon peel on top.

Gin Cocktail.—*(Use a large bar glass.)*

Fill up the glass with ice.
2 or 3 dashes of Gum Syrup.
2 or 3 dashes of Bitters.
1 dash of either Curacoa or Absinthe.
1 wine glass of Holland Gin.

Stir up well, strain into a fancy cocktail glass, squeeze a piece of lemon peel on top, and serve.

Whether Curacoa or Absinthe is taken depends on which the customer may desire.

Old Tom Gin Cocktail.—*(Use a large bar glass.)*

Fill the glass with fine shaved ice.
2 or 3 dashes of Gum Syrup.
1 or 2 dashes of Bitters.
1 or 2 dashes of Curacoa or Absinthe, if required.
1 wine glass of Old Tom Gin.

Stir up well with a spoon, strain into a cocktail glass, twist a piece of lemon peel on top, and serve.

Bottle of Cocktail for Parties.

1 qt. of good old Whiskey ; providing the bottle is large enough.
1 pony glass of Curacoa (red).
1 wine glass of Gum Syrup.
¾ pony glass of Bitters.

Mix this well by pouring it from one shaker into another, until it is thoroughly mixed; pour it into a bottle and cork it, put a label on it, and you will have an elegant bottle of Cocktail.

Japanese Cocktail. —*(Use a small bar glass.)*

Take 1 table-spoonful of Orgeat Syrup.
2 dashes of Bitters.
1 wine glass of Brandy.
1 or 2 pieces of lemon peel.
Fill the tumbler one-third with ice, stir well with a spoon, and strain into a cocktail glass.

Saratoga Cocktail.—*(Use a large bar glass.)*

¼ glass of fine shaved ice.
2 or 3 dashes of Pineapple Syrup.
2 or 3 dashes of Bitters.
2 or 3 dashes of Maraschino (di Zara).
¾ glass of fine old Brandy.
Mix well with a bar spoon and place 2 or 3 strawberries in a fancy cocktail glass, strain it, twist a piece of lemon peel over it, top it off with 1 squirt of Champagne, and serve.

Coffee Cocktail. —*(Use a large bar glass.)*

Take 1 tea-spoonful powdered white sugar.
1 fresh Egg.
1 large wine-glass of Port Wine.
1 pony of Brandy.
2 or 3 lumps of ice.
Break the egg into the glass, put in the sugar, and lastly the port wine, brandy and ice.
Shake up very thoroughly, and strain into a medium bar goblet. Grate a little nutmeg on top before serving.
The name of this drink is a misnomer, as coffee and bitters are not to be found among its ingredients, but it looks like coffee when it has been properly concocted, and hence probably its name.

Champagne Sour.—*(Use a fancy glass.)*

1 lump of Loaf Sugar.
2 dashes of fresh Lemon Juice.
Place the saturated sugar into a fancy glass, also a slice of orange and a slice of pineapple, a few strawberries or grapes (if in season), fill up the glass slowly with Champagne, and stir up well, and serve it.

Mint Julep.—*(Use a large bar glass.)*

1 table-spoonful of white pulverized Sugar.
2½ table-spoonfuls of water, mix well with a spoon.
1½ wine glass full of Brandy.

Take three or four sprigs of fresh mint, and press them well in the sugar and water, until the flavor of the mint is extracted; add the brandy, and fill the glass with fine shaved ice, then draw out the sprigs of mint and insert them in the ice with the stems downward, so that the leaves will be above, in the shape of a bouquet; arrange berries, and small pieces of sliced orange on top in a tasty manner, dash with Jamaica rum, and serve with a straw.

Gin Julep.—*(Use a large bar glass.)*

Made with the same ingredients as the Mint Julep, omitting the fancy fixings.

Brandy Julep.

Same as Mint Julep, without the fancy fixings.

Rum Julep.

Same as Mint Julep, using St. Croix or Santa Cruz Rum instead of brandy.

Champagne Julep.—*(Use a large bar glass.)*

1 lump of white sugar.
1 sprig Mint, press to extract the essence.
Pour the wine into the glass slowly, stirring gently continually.
Dress with sliced orange, grapes and berries, tastily, and serve.

Pineapple Julep.—*(For a party of six.)*

The juice of two Oranges.
1 gill of Raspberry Syrup.
1 gill of Maraschino.
1 gill of Old Tom Gin.
1 quart bottle Sparkling Moselle.
1 ripe Pineapple, peeled, sliced and cut up.
Put all the materials in a glass bowl; ice, and serve in flat glasses, ornamented with berries in season.

Whiskey Julep.—*(Use a large bar glass.)*

¼ table-spoonful of sugar.
½ wine glass full of Water or Selters.
3 or 4 sprigs of fresh Mint, dissolve well until all the essence of the Mint is extracted.
Fill up the glass with fine shaved ice.
1 wine glass full of Whiskey.
Stir up well with a spoon and ornament this drink with mint, oranges, pineapples and berries in a tasty manner; sprinkle a little sugar on top of it; dash with Jamaica rum, and serve.

Pousse Café.—*(Use a Sherry wine glass.)*

In mixing the above drink great care must be taken. As there are several liquors required, it should be made in such a manner that the portions will be perfectly separated from each other.

- $\frac{1}{6}$ glass of Parfait d'Amour or Raspberry syrup.
- $\frac{1}{6}$ glass of Maraschino.
- $\frac{1}{6}$ glass of Vanilla (green).
- $\frac{1}{6}$ glass of Curacoa (red).
- $\frac{1}{6}$ glass of Chartreuse (yellow).
- $\frac{1}{6}$ glass of Cognac (or Brandy).

The above ingredients will fill the glass.

Pousse L'Amour.—*(Use a Sherry wine glass.)*

This delicious French drink is somewhat similar to the Pousse Café, and also has to be carefully made; mix as follows:

- $\frac{1}{4}$ sherry glass of Maraschino; drop in
- 1 yolk of a fresh Egg.
- $\frac{1}{4}$ glass of Vanilla (green).
- $\frac{1}{4}$ glass of Cognac.

Proper attention must be paid that the yolk of the egg does not run into the liquor, in order to have it in its natural form.

Saratoga Pousse Café.—*(Use small wine glass.)*

- $\frac{1}{5}$ Curacoa.
- $\frac{1}{5}$ Benedictine.
- $\frac{1}{5}$ Raspberry Syrup.
- $\frac{2}{5}$ fine old Brandy.
- 1 tea-spoonful of vanilla cordial on top.

American Pousse Café.—*(Use small wine glass.)*

- $\frac{1}{4}$ Maraschino.
- $\frac{1}{4}$ Curacoa.
- $\frac{1}{4}$ Chartreuse (green).
- $\frac{1}{4}$ Brandy.

Keep the colors separate.

"Jersey Lily" Pousse Café.—*(Use pony glass.)*

Half fill with Chartreuse.
Half " " Brandy.

Pour brandy in carefully, so as not to disturb the Chartreuse, and serve.

Parisian Pousse Café.—*(Use small wine glass.)*

    Curacoa.
    Kirschwasser.
    Chartreuse.

Care should be observed to keep the ingredients from mixing together.

Faivre's Pousse Café.—*(Use small bar glass.)*

    ⅓ Parisian pousse café (as above).
    ⅓ Kirschwasser.
    ⅓ Curacoa.

Observe the directions given in the preceding recipe.

Brandy Crusta.—*(Use small bar glass.)*

    3 or 4 dashes of Gum Syrup.
    1 dash of Bitters.
    1 wine glass of Brandy.
    2 dashes of Curacoa.
    1 dash Lemon Juice.

Before mixing the above ingredients, prepare a cocktail glass as follows:

Rub a sliced lemon around the rim of the glass, and dip it in pulverized white sugar, so that the sugar will adhere to the edge of the glass. Pare half a lemon the same as you would an apple (all in one piece) so that the paring will fit in the wine glass. Put the above ingredients into a small whiskey glass filled one-third full of shaved ice, shake up well and strain the liquid into the cocktail glass prepared as above directed.

Whiskey and Gin Crustas are made in the same manner, using either of these liquors instead of Brandy.

Fancy Whiskey Smash.—*(Use a large bar glass.)*

    ½ tablespoonful of sugar.
    ½ glass of Water, or squirt of Selters.
    3 or 4 sprigs of mint, dissolve well with a spoon.
    Fill the glass full of fine shaved ice.
    1 wine glass of Whiskey.

Stir up well with a spoon; strain it into a fancy sour glass, ornament with fruit, and serve.

This drink requires particular care and attention, so as to have it palatable and look proper.

Mississippi Punch.—*(Use a large bar glass.)*

1 table-spoonful of Sugar.
½ wine glass of Water or Selters.
2 dashes of Lemon Juice, dissolved well.
½ wine glass of Jamaica Rum.
½ wine glass of Bourbon Whiskey.
1 wine glass of Brandy.

Fill the glass with shaved ice; shake or stir the ingredients well, ornament in a tasty manner with fruit in season, and serve with a straw.

Silver Fiz.—*(Use a large bar glass.)*

½ table-spoonful of Sugar.
2 or 3 dashes of Lemon Juice.
1 wine glass of Old Tom Gin, dissolved well, with a squirt of Vichy.
1 egg (the white only).
¾ glass filled with shaved ice.

Shake up well with a shaker, strain it into a good sized fiz glass, fill up the glass with Syphon Selters or Vichy water, mix well and serve.

This drink is a delicious one, and must be drank as soon as prepared, as it loses its strength and flavor.

Brandy Champarelle.—*(Use a Sherry wine glass.)*

¼ wine glass of Curaçoa (red).
¼ wine glass of Chartreuse (yellow).
¼ wine glass of Anisette.
¼ wine glass of Kirschwasser or Brandy,
whichever the customer desires, and serve.

Attention must be paid to prevent the different liquors from running into each other, to have them perfectly separated and distinct.

Champagne Cobbler.—*(Use a large bar glass.)*

¼ of a table-spoonful of Sugar.
¼ wine glass of Syphon Selters, dissolve well.
1 or 2 pieces of Orange.
1 or 2 pieces of Pineapple.
Fill the glass with ice.

Fill the balance with champagne, ornament the top in a tasty manner, and serve it with a straw.

This drink is generally mixed where they have champagne on draught, by having the champagne faucet screwed into the cork of the bottle.

Whiskey Daisy.—*(Use a large bar glass.)*

½ table-spoonful of Sugar.
2 or 3 dashes of Lemon Juice.
1 dash of Lime Juice.
1 squirt of Syphon Seltzer, dissolve with the lemon and Lime Juice.
¾ of the glass filled with fine shaved ice.
1 wine glass of good Whiskey.
Fill the glass with shaved ice.
½ pony glass Chartreuse (yellow).
Stir up well with a spoon, then take a fancy glass, have it dressed with fruit and strain the mixture into it, and serve.
This drink is very palatable and will taste good to most anybody.

Golden Slipper.—*(Use a wine glass.)*

½ wine glass Chartreuse (yellow).
1 yolk of an egg.
½ wine glass Danziger Goldwasser.
This is a favorite with American ladies, much relished.
Be careful when preparing this beverage not to disturb the yolk of the egg.

Sherry Cobbler.—*(Use a large bar glass.)*

½ table-spoonful of Sugar.
½ wine glass of water, dissolve with a spoon.
Fill the glass up with fine crystal ice.
Then fill the glass up with Sherry Wine.
Stir well with a spoon and ornament with grapes, oranges, pineapples, berries, etc., serve with a straw.

Whiskey Cobbler.—*(Use a large bar glass.)*

2 wine glasses Whiskey.
½ table-spoonful Sugar, dissolved well.
1½ table-spoonful Pineapple Syrup.
Fill glass with fine ice, stir well and dress with fruits;
serve with a straw.

Rhine Wine Cobbler.—*(Use a large bar glass.)*

 1½ table-spoonfuls of Sugar.
 1½ wine glass of Water, dissolve well with a spoon.
 1½ wine glass of Rhine Wine.
 Fill the glass with shaved ice.
Stir up well with a spoon; ornament with grapes, orange, pineapple, strawberries, in season, and serve with a straw.

 This is a fashionable German drink.

Catawba Cobbler.—*(Use a large bar glass.)*

 Take 1 teaspoonful of fine white Sugar, dissolved in a little water.
 1 slice of Orange cut into quarters.
Fill the glass half full of shaved ice, then fill it up with Catawba wine. Ornament the top with berries in season, and serve with a straw.

 Hock, Claret and Sauterne Cobblers are made the same way, substituting these liquors for the Catawba.

California Wine Cobbler.—*(Use a large bar glass.)*

 Fill glass with fine ice.
 ¾ table-spoonful Sugar.
 Juice of 1 Orange.
 1½ wine glass California Wine.
 Stir well; dress with fruit.
 Top with Port Wine. Serve with a straw.

Port Wine Cobbler.—*(Use a large bar glass.)*

 ½ table-spoonful of Sugar.
 1 pony glass of Orchard Syrup.
 ½ wine glass of Water, dissolve well with a spoon.
 Fill the glass with fine ice.
 1½ wine glass of Port Wine.
Mix up well, and ornament with grapes, berries, etc., in season, and serve.

Santinas New Orleans Pousse Café.—*(Use a Sherry wine glass.)*

 ⅓ wine glass Brandy.
 ⅓   "   Maraschino.
 ⅓   "   Curaçoa.
 Careful attention must be paid to the arrangement of colors, and to preventing the different portions from running into each other.

Arrack Punch.—*(Use a bar glass.)*

    1 table-spoon Sugar dissolved in a little water.
    1 or 2 dashes Lemon Juice.
    1 wine glass of Batavia arrack.
    ½ fill glass with fine ice.
Shake well. Dress with fruits, and serve with a straw.

Hot Arrack Punch.—*(Use a hot water glass.)*

    1 tea-spoon Sugar.
    1 or 2 dashes Lemon Juice.
    ¾ wine glass Arrack.
Fill up with hot water. Stir well; grate a little nutmeg on top, and serve.

Hot Boland Punch.

    1 lump Sugar.
    2 wine glasses boiling water.
    1   "   Scotch Whiskey.
    1 table-spoon Ginger Ale.

Brandy Punch.—*(Use a large bar glass.)*

    1 table-spoon Sugar dissolved in a little water.
    ½ of a small Lemon.
    ¼ wine glass St. Croix Rum.
    1½   "   Brandy.
    1 piece Pineapple.
    1 or 2 slices Orange.
Fill glass with fine ice. Shake well. Dress with fruits and serve with a straw.

Champagne Punch.—*(Serve in Champagne goblets.)*

    1 quart bottle Wine.
    ¼ lb. Sugar.
    1 Orange sliced.
    The Juice of 1 Lemon.
    3 or 4 slices of Pineapple.
    1 wine glass Strawberry Syrup.
Dress with fruit, and serve.

Claret Punch.—*(Use a large bar glass.)*

    1½ table-spoon Sugar.
    1 slice Lemon.
    2 slices Orange.
Fill glass with fine ice. Pour in claret wine. Shake well.
Dress with fruit in season, and serve with a straw.

Cosmopolitan Claret Punch.—*(Use a goblet.)*

    ½ filled with chopped Ice.
    1½ pony Brandy.
    ½ table-spoon Sugar.
    Fill with Claret.
Shake well and dress with berries and fruit, and serve.

Curacoa Punch.—*(Use a large bar glass.)*

    ¾ table-spoon Sugar.
    3 or 4 dashes Lemon Juice.
    1 wine glass Brandy.
    1 pony glass Curaçoa (red).
    ½ pony glass Jamaica Rum.
Dress with fruits as usual. Fill with fine ice and sip through
a straw.

Egg Milk Punch.—*(Use a large bar glass.)*

    1 Egg.
    ¾ table-spoon Sugar.
    1 wine glass Brandy.
    1 pony glass St. Croix Rum.
    ½ glass with fine Ice.
Fill up with milk—use the shaker in mixing—which must be
done thoroughly to a cream.
    Strain ; grate a little nutmeg on top, and it is ready.

Gin Punch.—*(Use a large bar glass.)*

    2 table-spoons white Sugar.
    1 pony Seltzer.
    1½ wine glass Holland Gin.
    4 or 5 dashes Lemon Juice.
Fill glass with fine ice.
    Shake well. Dress with 2 slices orange ; ½ slice pineapple,
and berries ; serve with a straw.

Hot Irish Punch.—*(Use a hot water glass.)*

1 or 2 lumps Sugar.
1 or 2 dashes of Lemon Juice.
1 wine glass Irish Whiskey.
Fill up with hot water; stir well.
Place a slice of lemon on top, grate a little nutmeg, and serve.

Kirschwasser Punch.—*(Use a large bar glass.)*

½ table-spoon Sugar.
2 or 3 dashes Lemon Juice.
3 or 4 dashes Chartreuse.
1 wine glass Kirschwasser.
Fill ¾ of the glass with fine ice.
Dress with Fruits; serve with a straw.

Medford Rum Punch.—*(Use a large bar glass.)*

Fill glass with fine ice.
¾ table-spoon Sugar.
2 or 3 dashes Lemon Juice.
1¼ glass Medford Rum.
1 dash of Jamaica Rum.
Stir well. Dress with fruits. Serve with a straw.

Milk Punch.—*(Use a large bar glass.)*

⅓ glass fine ice.
¾ table-spoon Sugar.
1 wine glass Brandy.
1 wine glass St. Croix Rum.
½ wine glass Jamaica Rum.
Fill up with fresh milk, mix well together, strain, and serve up,
with a little nutmeg on top.

Hot Milk Punch.—*(Use a large bar glass.)*

1 table-spoon of Sugar.
½ wine glass St. Croix Rum.
½ wine glass Brandy.
Fill the glass with Hot Milk.
Mix well with a spoon; grate nutmeg on top, and serve.
Always mix with a spoon. Never use the shaker to this.

Orchard Punch.—*(Use a large bar glass.)*

2 table-spoons Orchard Syrup.
2 or 3 dashes of Lime or Lemon Juice.
½ pony Pineapple Syrup.
Fill glass with fine ice.
1 wine glass California Brandy.
Stir well. Dress with fruits, dash with a little Port wine, and serve with a straw.

Orgeat Punch.—*(Use a large bar glass.)*

1½ table-spoon Orgeat Syrup.
1½ wine glass Brandy.
4 or 5 dashes Lemon.
Fill glass with fine ice.
Shake well. Dress with fruits; top off with a dash of Port wine. Serve with a straw.

Philadelphia Boating Punch.—*(Use a large bar glass.)*

Fill glass with fine ice.
1 table-spoon Sugar.
1 or 2 dashes Lemon Juice.
1 wine glass St. Croix Rum.
1 pony of Old Brandy.
Stir well. Dress with fruits, and serve with a straw.

Port Wine Punch.—*(Use a large bar glass.)*

½ table-spoon Sugar.
½ table-spoon Orchard Syrup.
1 or 2 dashes Lemon Juice.
1½ wine glass Port Wine.
Fill up with fine ice, stir well, and dress top with fruits in season. Serve with a straw.

Roman Punch.—*(Use a large bar glass.)*

½ fill glass with fine ice.
1 table-spoon Sugar.
2 or 3 dashes Lemon Juice.
Juice of half an Orange.
¼ pony Curaçoa.
½ wine glass Brandy.
½ pony glass Jamaica Rum.
Stir well. Dash with Port wine. Dress with fruit. Serve with a straw.

Sauterne Punch.

Is composed of the same ingredients as Claret Punch, but substituting Sauterne wine for claret.

7th Regiment Punch.—(*Use a large bar glass.*)

1 tablespoon Sugar.
2 or 3 dashes Lemon Juice.
1 wine glass Brandy.
1 wine glass Catawba Wine.

Flavor with raspberry syrup. Fill glass with fine ice; shake well. Dress with fruits. Dash with Jamaica rum and serve with a straw.

Sherry Wine Punch.—(*Use a large bar glass.*)

Fill glass with fine ice
2 wine glasses Sherry.
1 table-spoon Sugar.
2 or 3 dashes Lemon Juice.

Stir well. Dress with fruits and top off with a little claret. Serve with a straw.

69th Regiment Punch.—(*Use a hot whiskey glass.*)

½ wine glass Irish Whiskey.
½ wine glass Scotch Whiskey.
1 tea-spoon Sugar.
2 or 3 dashes Lemon Juice.
2 wine glasses Hot Water.

The imbibition of the above adds greatly to one's comfort on a cold night.

St. Charles Punch.—(*Use a large bar glass.*)

1 table-spoon Sugar.
¼ of Lemon Juice.
1 wine glass Port Wine.
1 pony glass Brandy.
1 wine glass Port Wine.

Fill with fine ice. Shake well. Dress top with fruits in season and serve with a straw.

St. Croix Rum Punch.—*(Use a large bar glass.)*

1 table-spoon Sugar.
3 or 4 dashes Lemon Juice.
¼ pony glass Jamaica Rum.
1 wine glass St. Croix Rum.
Fill up with fine ice. Dress top with fruit and berries. **Serve** with a straw.

Tip-Top Punch.—*(Use a large bar glass.)*

3 or 4 lumps of ice.
1 pony of Brandy.
1 lump of Sugar.
2 slices Pineapple.
2 slices Orange.
1 or 2 dashes Lemon Juice.
Fill with champagne. Stir well. Dress with fruits. **Serve** with a straw.

Vanilla Punch.

1 table-spoon Sugar dissolved in a little water.
3 or 4 dashes Lemon Juice.
2 or 3 dashes Curaçoa.
1 wine glass Brandy.
1 pony glass Vanilla Cordial.
Fill with fine ice. Mix well. Dress tastily with berries and fruit in season and serve with a straw. Or you can flavor with a little Vanilla extract instead of the cordial.

Hot Whiskey Punch.—*(Use a hct whiskey glass.)*

The juice of half a lemon, one or two lumps of sugar dissolved in one wine glass hot water.
2 wine glasses Scotch or Irish Whiskey.
Fill glass with boiling water and place on top a thin slice of lemon or a piece of the peel. Some grate a little nutmeg on top. Always place ice before the customer, and allow a spoon to remain in the drink, in order that the partaker of the beverage can help himself to ice, should the mixture be too hot for him.

Apple Punch.

In china bowl lay alternate layers of sliced apples and lemons, each layer being thickly strewed with powdered sugar, until the bowl is about half filled ; then pour a bottle of claret over the fruit and let it stand six hours. Pour it through a muslin bag, and it is ready for use.

Orange Punch.

¾ pint of Rum.
¾ pint of Brandy.
½ pint of Porter.
3½ pints of boiling Water.
¾ lb. Loaf Sugar.
4 Oranges.

Infuse the peel of 2, and the juice of 4 Oranges with the sugar in the water for ½ hour ; strain, and add the porter, rum and brandy. Sugar may be added, if it is desired sweeter.

A liquor glass of Curaçoa, Noyeau, or Maraschino is considered an improvement.

Instead of using both, rum and brandy, 1½ pints of either alone will answer.

This is also an excellent recipe for Lemon Punch by substituting lemons for oranges.

Rochester Punch.—*(For a small party.)*

2 bottles of sparkling Catawba.
2 bottles of sparkling Isabella.
1 bottle of Sauterne.
2 wine glasses of Maraschino.
2 wine glasses of Curaçoa,

Flavor with ripe strawberries. Should strawberries not be in season, add a few drops of extract of peach or vanilla. Ice in a cooler.

Absinthe Punch.—*(Use a large bar glass.)*

1 table-spoonful of Sugar.
1 wine glass of Absinthe.
Juice of ½ a lemon.
½ wine glass of Brandy.
1 table-spoonful of Orgeat Syrup.

Fill with ice, stir with spoon, ornament with orange, grapes and fruit in season.

Hot Brandy Punch.—*(Use a large beer glass.)*

1 wine glass of Cognac Brandy.
½ wine glass of Jamaica Rum.
2 table-spoonfuls of White Sugar.
½ of a lemon cut in small slices.

Fill glass with boiling water, stir well and grate nutmeg over the top,

Hot Scotch.—*(Use a small bar glass.)*

½ wine glass of good Scotch Whiskey, fill balance of glass with boiling water, drop in 1 lump of sugar and some thin yellow shavings of lemon peel ; stir well and serve.

Ale Punch.

1 quart of mild Ale.
1 glass of White Wine.
1 glass of Brandy.
1 glass of Capillaire.
1 Lemon.

Mix the ale, wine, brandy and Capillaire together with the juice of the lemon and a portion of the peel pared very thin. Grate nutmeg on the top, and add a bit of toasted bread.

Cider Punch.

½ pint of Sherry.
1 glass of Brandy.
1 bottle of Cider.
¼ pound of Sugar.
1 Lemon.

Pare the peel of half the lemon very thin ; pour the sherry upon it ; add the sugar, the juice of the lemon, and the cider, with a little grated nutmeg. Mix well and place it on ice. When cold, add the brandy and a few pieces of cucumber rind.

Maraschino Punch.—*(Use a large beer glass.)*

1 tea-spoonful of powdered Sugar, dissolved in a little water.
1 wine glass of Brandy.
2 dashes of Arrack.
½ pony glass of Maraschino.
The juice of half a small Lemon.

Fill the tumbler with shaved ice, shake well, ornament with fruit and berries in season, and serve with a straw.

Cold Whiskey Punch.—*(Use a large bar glass.)*

1 table-spoonful of powdered white Sugar, dissolved in a little water.
Juice of half a small Lemon.
1½ wine glasses of Irish or Scotch Whiskey.

Fill the glass with shaved ice, shake well, and dress the top with two thin slices of lemon, and berries in season. Serve with a straw.

Nectar Punch.

> 4½ pints of Rum.
> 2 quarts of Milk, boiling hot.
> 2 quarts of cold water.
> 2½ pounds of Loaf Sugar
> 15 Lemons.
> 1 nutmeg.

Cut off the peel of the lemons very thin and infuse them for forty-eight hours with a pint and a half of the rum. Add to the infusion the water, the juice of the lemons, the milk, and the nutmeg grated ; let it all stand for twenty-four hours, covered close ; then add the sugar, strain through flannel, and bottle for use. It is ready to use at any time.

Brandy and Rum Punch.—(Use a large bar glass.)

> 1 table-spoonful of powdered white Sugar, dissolved in a little water.
> 1 wine glass of Santa Cruz Rum.
> ½ wine glass of Brandy.
> Juice of half a small lemon.
> 1 slice of Orange (cut in quarters).
> 1 piece of Pineapple.

Fill the tumbler with shaved ice, shake well, and dress the top with sliced lime and berries in season. Serve with a straw.

El Dorado Punch.—(Use a large bar glass.)

> 1 pony of Brandy.
> ½ pony of Jamaica Rum.
> ½ pony of Bourbon.
> 1 table-spoonful of powdered sugar dissolved in a little water.
> A slice of Lemon.

Fill the tumbler with fine ice, shake well and ornament with berries or small pieces of orange. Serve with a straw.

Gothic Punch.—(Use a punch bowl.)

> 4 bottles of still Catawba Wine.
> 1 bottle of Claret.
> 1 bottle of Champagne.
> 3 Oranges.
> 10 table-spoonfuls of Sugar.

Dissolve the sugar in the Catawba and Claret wines ; add the juice of the oranges. When mixed, put it in ice for an hour or more, and then add the Champagne.

Punch Grassot.—*(Use a large goblet.)*

> 1   wine glass of Brandy.
> 1   tea-spoonful of Curaçoa.
> 1   drop of Acetic Acid.
> 2   tea-spoonfuls of simple Syrup.
> 1   tea-spoonful of Strawberry Syrup.
> ¼ of a pint of Water.
> Half a small Lemon, sliced.

Mix, serve up with ice, in large goblet, and, if possible, garnish the top with a slice of peach or apricot. In cold weather this punch is admirable served hot.

This recipe is credited to M. Grassot, of the Palais Royal, France.

Regent's Punch.—*(Use a punch bowl.)*

> 1½ pint of strong Green Tea (hot).
> 1½ pint of Lemon Juice.
> 1½ pint of Capillaire.
> 1 · pint of Jamaica Rum.
> 1   pint of Brandy.
> 1   pint of Batavia Arrack.
> 1   pint of Curaçoa.
> 1   bottle of Champagne.
> 1   Pineapple, sliced.
> 2   Oranges, sliced.

Mix the ingredients well together in a punch-bowl, and add the wine and ice just before serving.

Tea Punch.—*(Use a heated metal bowl.)*

> ½ pint of good Brandy.
> ½ pint of Rum.
> ¼ pound of Loaf-Sugar, dissolved in water.
> 1   ounce of best Green Tea.
> 1   quart of boiling water
> 1   large Lemon.

Infuse the tea in the Water. Warm a silver or other metal bowl until quite hot; place in it the brandy, rum, sugar, and the juice of the lemon. The oil of the lemon peel should be first obtained by rubbing with a few lumps of the sugar. Set the contents of the bowl on fire; and while flaming, pour in the tea gradually, stirring with a ladle. It will continue to burn for some time, and should be ladled into glasses while in that condition. A heated metal bowl will cause the punch to burn longer than if a china bowl is used.

Canadian Punch.—*(For a small party.)*

2 quarts of Rye Whiskey.
1 pint of Jamaica Rum.
6 Lemons, sliced.
1 pineapple, sliced.
4 quarts of water.

Sweeten to taste, and ice before serving.

Spread Eagle Punch.—*(For a social party.*

1 bottle of Islay Whiskey.
1 bottle of Monongahela.

Lemon peel, sugar and—boiling water at discretion.

Century Club Punch.—

1 pint old Santa Cruz Rum.
1 pint of old Jamaica Rum.
5 pints of water.

With the addition of lemon juice and sugar to suit the taste, this makes a nice punch.

Pineapple Punch.—*(For a party of ten.)*

4 bottles of Champagne.
1 pint of Jamaica Rum.
1 pint of Brandy.
1 gill of Curaçoa.
Juice of four Lemons.
2 Pineapples sliced.

Sweeten to taste with pulverized white sugar.

Put the pineapple with quarter of a pound of sugar in a glass bowl, and let them stand until the sugar is well soaked in the pineapple, then add all the other ingredients, except the Champagne.

Let this mixture stand in ice for about an hour, then add the Champagne, and ornament with sliced orange, and other fruits in season.

Serve in Champagne glasses.

Pineapple punch is sometimes made by adding sliced pineapple to brandy punch.

Imperial Punch. —*(One quart of punch.)* .

1 bottle of Claret.
1 bottle of Soda Water.
4 table-spoonfuls of powdered white Sugar, dissolved in
a little of the Soda Water.
¼ tea-spoonful of grated Nutmeg.
1 liqueur-glass of Maraschino.
About ½ pound of Ice.
3 or 4 slices of Cucumber Rind.
Put all the ingredients into a pitcher and mix well.

Royal Punch.—*(For a small party.)*

1 pint of hot Green Tea.
½ pint of Brandy.
½ pint of Jamaica Rum.
1 wine glass of Curaçoa.
1 wine glass of Arrack.
Juice of two Limes.
A slice of Lemon.
White Sugar to taste.
1 gill of warm Calf's Foot Jelly.
To be drunk as hot as possible.

This is a composition worthy of a king, and the materials are
admirably blended; the inebriating effects of the spirits being
deadened by the tea. Whilst the jelly softens the mixture, and
destroys the acrimony of the acid and sugar.

The whites of a couple of eggs well beat up to a froth, may
be substituted for the jelly where that is not at hand.

If the punch is too strong, add more green tea to taste.

United Service Punch.—

½ pint of Arrack.
1 pint of Jamaica Rum.
½ pound of Loaf Sugar.
3 pints of hot Tea.
6 Lemons.
Rub off the peel of four of the lemons with some of the sugar.
Dissolve the sugar in the tea; add the juice of all the lemons,
and the Arrack. Serve cold.

Fedora.—*(Use a large bar glass.)* •

> 1 pony of Brandy.
> 1 pony of Curaçoa.
> ½ pony of Jamaica Rum.
> ½ pony of Bourbon.
> 1 table-spoonful of powdered sugar, dissolved in a little
>   water.
> 1 slice of Lemon.

Fill the tumbler with fine ice; shake well and ornament with
berries or small pieces of orange, serve with a straw.

Ale Sangaree.—*(Use a large bar glass.)*

> 1 tea-spoonful of Sugar.
> ½ wine glass of water, dissolve with a spoon.

Fill up the balance with Ale, grate a little nutmeg on top, and
serve.

It is customary to ask the customer if he desires Old, New or
Mixed Ale; if he desires New Ale, you must prevent the foam
from running over the glass; attention must also be paid to
the temperature of the Ale, so as to have it not too cold or too
warm.

Brandy Sangaree.—*(Use a small bar glass.)*

> 1 or 2 lumps of ice.
> ½ wine glass of water.
> ½ table-spoonful of Sugar.
> 1 glass of Brandy.

Stir up well with a spoon; grate a little nutmeg on top, and
serve; strain if desired.

Gin Sangaree.

> ½ tea-spoon sugar dissolved in a little water.
> 1 wine glass Holland Gin.
> 1 lump of ice.

Stir with a spoon; put about a tea-spoon of sherry on top, and
serve.

Porter Sangaree.—*(Use a large bar glass.)*

> ½ table-spoon sugar.
> 3 or 4 lumps of ice.
> Fill up with porter.

Stir well; remove the ice; grate nutmeg on top, and serve.

Porteree.

> Same as above.

Port Wine Sangaree.—*(Use a small bar glass.)*

1 or 2 lumps ice.
1 tea-spoon sugar.
1½ wine glass Port Wine.

Shake well; remove ice; grate a little nutmeg on top; serve.

Sherry Sangaree.—*(Use a medium bar glass.)*

1 claret glass of Sherry Wine.
½ tea-spoonful of fine white sugar.
2 or 3 small lumps of ice.

Shake up well, strain into a small bar glass, serve with a little grated nutmeg.

Quince Liqueur.—*(One and a half gallons.)*

2 quarts of Quince Juice.
4 quarts of Cognac Brandy.
2½ pounds of white sugar.
12 ounces of bitter Almonds, *bruised.*
1 pound of Coriander-Seeds.
36 Cloves.

Grate a sufficient number of quinces to make two quarts of juice, and squeeze them through a jelly-bag. Mix the ingredients all together, and put them into a demijohn, and shake well every day for ten days. Then strain the liquid through a jelly-bag till it is perfectly clear, and bottle for use.

Applejack Sour.—*(Use a large bar glass.)*

½ table-spoonful of sugar.
2 or 3 dashes of Lemon Juice.
1 squirt of Syphon Selters water, dissolve well.
¾ glass of fine shaved ice.
1 wine glass of old Cider Brandy or what they call Apple Jack.

Stir up with a spoon, strain it into a sour glass, and ornament it with a little fruit, and serve.

Brandy Sour.—*(Use a large bar glass.)*

Fill glass with ice.
½ table-spoon sugar.
2 or 3 dashes Lemon Juice.
A squirt of Seltzer.
1 wine glass Brandy.

Stir well; strain into a sour glass; dress with fruits as usual, and serve.

Continental Sour.

½ tea-spoon sugar, dissolved in water.
Juice of ½ a Lemon.
1 wine glass Whiskey or liquor as desired; fine ice; shake well, and strain into a sour glass, and dash with claret.

Egg Sour.

1 table-spoon powdered sugar.
3 lumps of ice.
1 egg.
Juice of 1 Lemon.
Shake thoroughly; serve with straw; nutmeg grated on top.

Gin Sour.—*(Use a large bar glass.)*

½ table-spoonful of sugar.
2 or 3 dashes of Lemon Juice.
1 dash of Lime Juice.
1 squirt of Syphon Selters water.
Dissolve the sugar and lemon well with a spoon.
¾ filled with fine shaved ice.
1 wine glass of Holland Gin.
Mix well, strain it into a sour glass, dress with a little fruit in season, and serve.

Jersey Sour.—*(Use a small bar glass.)*

1 large tea-spoonful of powdered white sugar dissolved in a little water.
2 or 3 dashes of Lemon Juice.
1 wine glass of Apple Jack.
Fill the glass with shaved ice, shake up, and strain into a claret glass. Ornament with berries.

St. Croix Sour.—*(Use a large bar glass.)*

½ table-spoon sugar, dissolved in a little Seltzer water.
¼ of a Lemon squeezed into the glass.
½ glass fine ice.
1 wine glass St. Croix Rum.
Stir well; strain into a sour glass; dress with fruit in season, and serve.

Jamaica Rum Sour.—*(Use a large bar glass.)*

½ table-spoonful of sugar.
2 or 3 dashes of Lemon Juice.
1 squirt of Syphon Selters, dissolve well.
¾ glass of fine shaved ice.
1 wine glass of Jamaica Rum.
Stir well with a spoon, strain into a sour glass, ornament with fruit, and serve.

Whiskey Sour.—*(Use a large bar glass.)*

½ table-spoonful of sugar.
3 or 4 dashes of Lemon Juice.
1 squirt of Syphon Selters water, dissolve the sugar and lemon well with a spoon.
Fill the glass with ice.
1 wine glass of Whiskey.
Stir up well, strain into a sour glass; place your fruit into it, and serve.

Santa Cruz Sour.—*(Use a small bar glass.)*

1 large tea-spoonful of white sugar dissolved in a little Seltzer or Apollinaris water.
3 dashes of Lemon Juice.
1 wine glass of Santa Cruz Rum.
Fill the glass full of shaved ice, shake up and strain into a claret glass, ornament with orange and berries in season.

White Lion.—*(Use a small bar glass.)*

1 tea-spoonful of pulverized white sugar.
½ a lime (squeeze out juice and put rind in glass).
1 wine glass Santa Cruz Rum.
1 tea-spoonful of Curacoa.
1 tea-spoonful of Raspberry Syrup.
Fill the glass half-full of shaved ice, shake up well and strain into a cocktail glass.

Rock and Rye.—*(Use a whiskey glass.)*

This drink must be very carefully prepared, and care must be taken to procure the best Rock Candy Syrup, and also the best of Rye Whiskey, as this drink is an effective remedy for sore throats, etc.

In serving Rock and Rye, put ½ table-spoonful of Rock Candy Syrup into the glass, place a spoon in it, and hand the bottle of Rye Whiskey to the customer, to help himself.

Brandy Shrub.—*(To make three quarts.)*

2 quarts of Brandy.
1 quart of Sherry.
2 pounds of loaf sugar dissolved in sufficient water.
5 Lemons.

Peel the rinds of 2 of the lemons, add the juice of all five, and mix with the brandy. Cover it close for three days; then add the sherry and sugar, strain through a jelly-bag and bottle.

Rum Shrub.—*(To make nearly five gallons.)*

3 gallons best Jamaica Rum.
1 quart of Orange Juice.
1 pint of Lemon Juice.
6 pounds of powdered sugar dissolved in sufficient water.
3 pints of fresh Milk.

Mix together all but the milk, and let them remain closely covered over night. Next day boil the milk; and when cold, add it to the mixture. Filter through a flannel bag lined with blotting paper, and bottle, corking immediately.

Raspberry Shrub.—*(Use a bowl for mixing.)*

1 quart of Vinegar.
3 quarts of ripe Raspberries.

After standing a day, strain it, adding to each pint a pound of sugar, and skim it clear, while boiling about half an hour.

Put a wine glass of brandy to each pint of the shrub, when cool.

Two spoonfuls of this, mixed with a tumbler of water, is an excellent drink in warm weather and during a fever.

John Collins.—*(Use an extra large bar glass.)*

¼ table-spoonful of sugar.
2 or 3 dashes of Lemon Juice.
2 dashes of Lime Juice.
4 or 5 small lumps of ice.
1 wine glass of Holland Gin.

Pour in a bottle of plain soda, mix up well, remove the ice and serve.

Care must be taken not to let the foam of the soda water run over the glass while pouring it in. This drink must be taken as soon as mixed, or it will lose its flavor.

Hot Rum.—*(Use a hot water glass.)*

    1 or 2 lumps of loaf sugar, dissolve with a little hot water.
    1 wine glass of Jamaica Rum.

Fill the balance with hot water, stir up well with a spoon, grate a little nutmeg on top and serve.

    The genuine Jamaica Rum only should be used, in order to make this drink palatable.

Hot Spiced Rum.—*(Take a hot water glass.)*

    1 or 2 lumps of loaf sugar.
    ½ tea-spoonful of mixed allspice; dissolve with a little hot water.
    1 wine glass of Jamaica Rum.

Fill up the balance of the glass with hot water, mix well and grate a little nutmeg on top, and serve.

Brandy and Ginger Ale.—*(Use a large soda water glass.)*

    1 wine glass of Brandy.
    2 or 3 small lumps of ice.

Fill up the glass with Irish ginger ale.

St. Croix Crusta.—*(Use a large bar glass.)*

    Take a nice clean lemon, the same size as your wine glass, cut off both ends, and peel it the same as you would an apple, put the lemon peel in the glass, so that it will line the entire inside of the glass, dip the edge of the glass and the lemon peel in pulverized sugar and mix as follows :

    3 or 4 dashes of Orchard Syrup.
    1 dash of Bitters.
    ½ glass of fine ice.
    1 small dash of Lemon Juice.
    2 dashes of Maraschino.
    1 wine glass of St. Croix Rum.

Mix well with a spoon, and strain into a wine glass, dress with small pieces of pineapple and strawberries, and serve.

Champagne Velvet.—*(Use a large sized goblet.)*

    For this drink a bottle of Champagne and a bottle of Irish Porter must be opened. It is mixed as follows :

    Fill the glass ½ full with Porter, the balance with Champagne.

    Stir up with a spoon slowly, and you have what is called Champagne Velvet, because it will make you feel within a short time as fine as silk.

    It is rather an expensive drink, but a good one.

Bottled Velvet.—*(Use a punch bowl.)*

    1 bottle of Moselle.
    ½ pint of Sherry.
    2 table-spoonfuls of sugar.
    1 Lemon.
    1 sprig of Verbena.
Peel the lemon very thin, using only sufficient of the peel to
produce the desired flavor; add the other ingredients; strain
and ice.

Soda Negus.—*(Use a small punch bowl; about one quart.)*

    1 pint of Port Wine.
    12 lumps of white loaf sugar.
    8 cloves.
    Grated Nutmeg, sufficient to fill a small tea-spoon.
Put the above ingredients into a thoroughly clean sauce pan,
warm and stir them well, but do not suffer it to boil; upon the
warm wine empty a bottle of plain soda water. This makes a
delicious and refreshing drink.

Brandy and Gum.—*(Use a large whiskey glass.)*

    1 or 2 dashes Gum Syrup.
    1 or 2 lumps ice.
  Place a spoon in the glass, and hand with a bottle of brandy
to the customer.

English Bishop.—*(Use a small punch bowl to make one quart.)*

    1 quart of Port Wine.
    1 Orange (stuck pretty well with cloves, the quantity
        being a matter of taste).
Roast the orange before a fire, and when sufficiently brown, cut
in quarters, and pour over it a quart of Port Wine (previously
made hot), add sugar to taste, and let the mixture simmer over
the fire for half an hour.

Brandy Scaffa.—*(Use a Sherry glass.)*

    ¼ sherry glass of Raspberry syrup.
    ¼ sherry glass of Maraschino.
    ¼ sherry glass of Chartreuse (green).
Top it off with Brandy, and serve.
    This drink must be properly prepared to prevent the different
colors from running into each other, each must appear separate.

Balaklava Nectar.—*(For a party of fifteen.)*

Thinly peel the rind of ½ lemon, shred it fine and put it in a punch bowl, add 4 table-spoonfuls of crushed sugar and the juice of

    1 Lemon.
    1 gill of Maraschino.
    2 bottles of Soda water.
    2 bottles of Claret.
    2 bottles of Champagne.

Stir well together and dress the top with fruit in season, and serve.

Bishop.—*(Use a large bar glass.)*

    1 table-spoon Sugar.
    2 dashes Lemon Juice.
    Half the juice of an Orange.
    One squirt Seltzer water.
    ¾ glass filled with fine ice.
    Fill the balance with Burgundy.
    Dash of Jamaica Rum.

Stir well. Dress with fruit, and serve with a straw.

Hari-Kari.

Make a whiskey sour large enough to half fill a brandy glass or tumbler when strained, and fill with seltzer or vichy to suit the party.

Dress with fruits in season.

Brandy, burned, and Peach.—*(Use a small bar glass.)*

    1 wine-glass Brandy.
    ½ table-spoon Sugar.
    Burn Brandy and sugar together in a dish or saucer.
    2 or 3 slices dried peach.

Place the fruit in the glass, pour the burned liquid over it, grate a little nutmeg on top, and serve.

The above is a Southern preparation, and often used in cases of diarrhœa.

Sherry Wine and Ice.—*(Use a whiskey glass.)*

    1 or 2 lumps of broken ice.

Place a bar spoon into the glass, hand this out with the bottle of Sherry wine, and let the customer help himself.

If a hotel, restaurant or café is attached to the establishment and the customer should call for such drink at the table, it is the bartender's duty to fill the glass with Sherry wine, and not send the bottle to the table, unless requested to do so.

Columbia Skin.—*(Use a small bar glass.)*

> 1 tea-spoonful of sugar, dissolve well with a little water.
> 1 slice of Lemon.
> 2 or 3 pieces of broken ice.
> 1 wine glass of Rum.

Stir up well with a spoon; grate a little nutmeg on top and serve.

Gin and Milk.—*(Use a whiskey glass.)*

Hand the bottle of Gin, glass and spoon out to the customer to help himself, fill up the balance with good, rich ice cold milk, stir up with a spoon and you will have a very nice drink.

Gin and Wormwood.—*(Use a small bar glass.)*

Take six to eight sprigs of wormwood, put these in a quart bottle and fill up with Holland gin, leave this stand for a few days, until the essence of the wormwood is extracted into the gin. In handing out this, pour a little of the above into a small whiskey glass and hand it with the bottle of gin to the customer to help himself.

This drink is popular in the eastern part of the country, where the wormwood is used as a substitute for bitters.

Brandy Daisy.

> ½ table-spoonful of sugar.
> 2 or 3 dashes of Lemon Juice.
> 1 squirt of Selters water, dissolve well with a spoon.
> ½ glass of Chartreuse (yellow).
> Fill up the glass with fine ice.
> 1 glass of Brandy.

Stir up well with a spoon, place the fruit into a fancy bar glass, strain the ingredients into it, and serve.

Soda and Nectar.—*(Use a large bar glass.)*

> 3 or 4 dashes of Lemon Juice.
> ¾ of a glass of water.
> ½ tea-spoonful of bicarbonate of soda, with sufficient white sugar to sweeten nicely.

When mixed, put in the plain soda, stir well, and drink while in foaming state.

This is an excellent morning drink to regulate the bowels,

Stone Wall.—*(Use a large bar glass.)*

    ¼ table-spoonful of sugar.
    3 or 4 lumps of ice.
    1 wine glass of Whiskey.
    1 bottle of plain Soda water.
Stir up well with a spoon, remove the ice and serve.
  This is a very cooling drink, and generally called for in the warm season.

Stone Fence.—*(Use a whiskey glass.)*

    Fill glass with fine ice.
    ½ table-spoon sugar.
    3 or 4 dashes Lemon Juice.
    ½ wine glass Seltzer water.
    1 wine-glass Whiskey.

Shandy Gaff.—*(Use a large bar glass.)*

  Fill the glass half full of Old Ale or Bass Ale, and the other half with Belfast Ginger Ale; stir up with a spoon, and serve.

How to Mix Tom and Jerry.—*(Use a punch bowl for the mixture.)*

  Use eggs according to quantity. Before using eggs, be careful and have them fresh and cold; go to work and take two bowls, break up your eggs very carefully, without mixing the yolk with the whites, but have the whites in a separate bowl, take an egg beater and beat the white of the eggs in such a manner that it becomes a stiff froth; add 1½ table-spoonfuls of sugar for each egg, and mix this thoroughly together, and then beat the yolks of the eggs until they are as thin as water; mix the yolks of the eggs with the whites and sugar together, until the mixture gets the consistency of a light batter, and it is necessary to stir the mixture up every little while to prevent the eggs from separating.

How to Serve Tom and Jerry.—*(Use either a mug or a bar glass.)*

    2 table-spoonfuls of the above mixture.
    1 wine glass of Brandy.
    1 pony glass of Jamaica rum.
Fill the mug or glass with hot water or hot milk, and stir up well with a spoon, then pour the mixture from one mug to the other, three or four times, until the above ingredients are thoroughly mixed, grate a little nutmeg on top, and serve.

Hot Whiskey.—*(Use a hot whiskey glass.)*

Place a bar-spoon into the glass before pouring in hot water, to avoid cracking the glass, and have a separate glass filled with fine ice, which must be placed in a convenient position, so that if the customer finds his drink too hot, he can help himself to a little ice; the bartender should at all times handle the sugar with a pair of tongues.   Mix as follows:

1 or 2 lumps of loaf sugar, with a little hot water to dissolve the sugar well.

1 wine glass of Scotch Whiskey.

Fill the glass with hot water; then mix well; squeeze and throw in the lemon peel, grate a little nutmeg on top and serve.

It is customary to use Scotch Whiskey in preparing this drink, unless otherwise desired by the customer.

Beef Tea.—*(Use a hot water glass.)*

¼ tea-spoonful of the best Beef Extract.

Fill the glass with hot water; stir up well with a spoon, and hand this to the customer, place pepper, salt and celery salad handy, and if the customer should require it, put in a small quantity of Sherry wine or Brandy.

Fine Lemonade for Parties.—*(Use a punch bowl, one gallon.)*

Take the rind of 8 Lemons.

Juice of 12 Lemons.

2 lbs. of loaf sugar.

1 gallon of boiling water.

Rub the rinds of the 8 lemons on the sugar until it has absorbed all the oil from them, and put it with the remainder of the sugar into a jug; add the lemon juice and pour the boiling water over the whole.   When the sugar is dissolved, strain the lemonade through a piece of muslin, and when cool, it will be ready for use.   The lemonade will be much improved by having the whites of 4 eggs beaten up with it.   A larger or smaller quantity of this lemonade may be made by increasing or diminishing the quantity of the ingredients.

Hot Lemonade.—*(Use a large bar glass.)*

1 table-spoonful of sugar.

7 or 8 dashes of Lemon Juice.

Fill up the glass with hot water, stir up with a spoon and serve.

Rhine Wine and Seltzer.—*(Use a large wine glass).*

The bartender's attention is called to the fact, that when a customer calls for Rhine Wine and Seltzer water, he desires a larger portion of wine than of Seltzer; and if he should call for Seltzer and wine, he desires more Seltzer than wine; attention must be paid that both the wine and the Seltzer are continually kept on ice.

This is a favorite drink with German people, and preferred by them in many cases to lemonade.

Tom Collins Brandy.—*(Use a large bar glass.)*

5 or 6 dashes of Gum Syrup.
1 or 2 dashes of Maraschino.
Juice of small Lemon.
1 wine glass Brandy.
1 or 2 lumps of ice.

Fill up with plain soda. Do not shake if the soda is cold.

Tom Collins Gin and Whiskey.

Are concocted same as the brandy, substituting their respective liquors.

Lemonade.—*(Use a large bar glass.)*

1½ table-spoonful of sugar.
6 to 8 dashes of Lemon juice.
¾ glass filled with shaved ice.

Fill the balance with water; shake or stir well; dress with fruit in season, and serve with a straw.

To make this drink taste pleasant, it must be at all times good and strong; therefore take plenty of lemon juice and sugar.

Seltzer Lemonade.—*(Use a large bar glass.)*

1½ table-spoonful of sugar.
4 to 6 dashes of Lemon Juice.
4 or 5 small lumps of broken ice.

Then fill up the glass with Syphon Seltzer, stir up well with a spoon, and serve.

If customers desire to have the imported Seltzer waters, use that instead of the Syphon Seltzer.

In order to have the above drink mixed properly you must not spare sugar or lemon juice.

Soda Lemonade.—*(Use a large bar glass.)*

    1 table-spoonful of Sugar.
    6 to 8 dashes of Lemon Juice.
    3 or 4 lumps of broken ice.
    1 bottle of plain Soda water.
Stir up well with a spoon, remove the ice, and serve.
    Open the soda beneath the counter, to avoid squirting part of it over the customer.

Orgeat Lemonade.—*(Use a large bar glass.)*

    1½ wine-glass of Orgeat Syrup.
    ½ table-spoonful of Sugar.
    6 to 8 dashes of Lemon Juice.
    ¾ glass of shaved ice.
    Fill the glass with water.
Mix up well and ornament with grapes, berries, etc., in season, and serve with a straw.
    This is a fine drink in warm climates.

Italian Wine Lemonade.—*(Use a large bar glass.)*

    1 table-spoon Sugar, dissolved in a little water.
    4 or 5 dashes Lemon Juice.
    ½ glass filled with fine ice.
    1 wine-glass Sherry, Claret or Port Wine.
Fill up with water; stir well; dress top with fruits, and serve with a straw.

Orange Lemonade.—*(Use a large bar glass.)*

    ¾ glass fine ice.
    1 table-spoon Sugar.
    Juice of 1 Orange.
    1 or 2 dashes Lemon Juice.
Fill up with water; shake and dress with fruit. Serve with a straw.

Rhine Wine Lemonade.—*(Use a goblet.)*

    1 table-spoon Sugar.
    Juice of ½ a Lemon.
A little ice, and fill up with Rhine wine, dress with fruit in season, and serve.

Saratoga or Sea Breeze Egg Lemonade.—*(Use a large bar glass.)*

1 Egg.
1 table-spoon Sugar.
½ the juice of Lemon.

Fill ¾ of the glass with fine ice; balance with water; use the shaker until well mixed; strain and serve; grate a little nutmeg on top.

Orangeade.

This agreeable beverage is made the same way as lemonade, substituting oranges for lemons.

Draught Lemonade, or Lemon Sherbet.

5 Lemons, sliced.
4 oz. lump sugar.
1 qt. boiling water.

A Cheaper Method.

1½ oz. Cream of Tartar.
1½ oz. Tartaric or Citric Acid.
Juice and peel of three Lemons.
2 lbs. or more loaf sugar.

The sweetening must be regulated according to taste.

Imperial Drink for Families.

3 oz. Cream of Tartar.
Juice and peel of 3 or 4 Lemons.
2 lbs. coarse sugar.

Put these into a gallon pitcher and pour on boiling water. When cool, it will be fit for use.

Sherbet.

10 oz. Carbonate of Soda.
8 oz. Tartaric Acid.
3 lbs. loaf sugar, finely powdered.
4 dr. Essence of Lemon.

Let the powders be very dry. Mix them intimately and keep them for use in a wide mouthed bottle closely corked.

Put two good sized tea-spoonfuls into a tumbler: pour in half a pint of cold water, stir briskly, and drink off.

Lemonade Powders.

1 lb. finely powdered loaf sugar.
1 oz. Tartaric or Citric Acid.
20 drops Essence of Lemon.

Mix, and keep very dry.

Two or three tea-spoonfuls of this stirred briskly in a tumbler of water, will make a very pleasant glass of lemonade. If effervescent lemonade be desired, ½ oz. of Carbonate of Soda must be added to the above.

Nectar.

1 dr. Citric Acid.
1 sc. Bicarbonate of Potash.
1 oz. white sugar, powdered.

Fill a soda-water bottle nearly full of water, drop in the potash and sugar, and lastly the Citric Acid. Cork the bottle up immediately and shake. As soon as the crystals are dissolved the nectar is fit for use. It may be colored with a small portion of cochineal.

Raspberry, Strawberry, Currant, or Orange Effervescing Draughts.

Take one quart of the juice of either of the above fruits, filter it, and boil it into a syrup, with one pound of powdered loaf sugar. To this add one ounce and a half of Tartaric Acid. When cold put it into a bottle and keep it well corked. When required, fill a half pint tumbler three-parts full of water, and add two table-spoonfuls of the syrup. Then stir in briskly a small tea-spoonful of carbonate of soda. The color may be improved by adding a small portion of cochineal to the syrup at the time of boiling.

Mulled Wine.—*(Use a punch bowl.)*

2½ pints of good Sherry Wine.
2 pints hot water.
¼ pound of sugar.
Whites of 12 Eggs.

Dissolve the sugar in the water, add the wine, and let the mixture come nearly to the boil. Meantime beat up the *whites* of the eggs to a froth, pour them into the hot mixture, stirring rapidly, and add a little nutmeg.

The vessel in which the wine is boiled must be *thoroughly* clean.

Mulled Wine with Eggs.—*(Use a punch bowl.)*

> 9 fresh Eggs.
> 4 table-spoonfuls of powdered white sugar.
> 1 quart either of Port, Claret or red Burgundy wine.
> Grated nutmeg to taste.
> 1 pint of water.

Beat up the whites and the yolks of the eggs separately, the sugar with the yolks. Pour into a *delicately clean* skillet the wine and half a pint of water, set this on the fire. Mix the whites and yolks of the eggs in the bowl with the balance of the water and beat them together thoroughly. When the wine boils pour it on the mixture in the bowl, add the nutmeg, and stir it rapidly.

Be careful not to pour the mixture into the wine, or the eggs will curdle.

Some persons may prefer more sugar, and the addition of a little allspice, but that is a matter of taste.

Mulled Wine without Eggs.—*(General rule for making.)*

To every pint of Wine allow :
> 1 small tumblerful of water.
> Sugar and spice to taste.

In making preparations like the above, it is very difficult to give the exact proportions of ingredients like sugar and spice, as what quantity might suit one person would be to another quite distasteful.

Boil the spice in the water until the flavor is extracted, then add the wine and sugar, and bring the whole to the boiling point, then serve with strips of crisp, dry toast, or with biscuits.

The spices usually used for mulled wine are cloves, grated nutmeg, and cinnamon.

Any kind of wine may be mulled, but Port or Claret are those usually selected for the purpose ; and the latter requires a large proportion of sugar.

The vessel that the wine is boiled in must be delicately clean.

Mulled Cider.

Cider may be mulled in precisely the same manner as recommended in the preceding recipe, omitting the water, and using twice the quantity of cider for the same number of eggs.

Brandy Flip.—*(Use a large bar glass.)*

1 fresh Egg.
¾ table-spoonful of sugar.
¾ glass of shaved ice.
1 wine glass full of Brandy.

Shake the above ingredients well in a shaker, strain into a flip or other fancy bar glass, and grate a little nutmeg on top and serve

---

Whiskey Flip.

Same as above, substituting Whiskey for Brandy.

Hot Brandy Flip.—*(Use large bar glass, heated.)*

1 tea-spoonful of sugar.
1 wine glass of Brandy.
Yolk of one egg.

Dissolve the sugar in a little hot water, add the brandy and egg, shake up thoroughly, pour into a medium bar glass, and fill it one-half full of boiling water. Grate a little nutmeg on top, and serve.

Hot Rum Flip.—*(Use large bar glass, heated.)*

Same as Brandy Flip, substituting Jamaica Rum instead of Brandy.

Hot Whiskey Flip.

Same as Brandy Flip, using Whiskey instead of Brandy.

Hot Gin Flip.

Same as Brandy Flip, using Holland Gin instead of Brandy.

Cold Rum Flip.—*(Use large bar glass.)*

1 tea-spoonful powdered sugar, dissolved in a little water.
1 wine glass Jamaica Rum.
1 fresh Egg.
2 or 3 lumps of ice.

Shake up thoroughly, strain in a medium glass, and grate a little nutmeg on top.

Cold Whiskey Flip.—*(Use a large bar glass.)*

Same as Rum Flip, substituting Bourbon or Rye Whiskey instead of Jamaica Rum.

Sherry Flip.—*(Use a large bar glass.)*

1 fresh Egg.
½ table-spoonful of sugar.
½ glassful of shaved ice.
1½ wine glass full of Sherry Wine.

Shake it well, until it is thoroughly mixed, strain it into a fancy bar glass, grate a little nutmeg on top and serve.

This is a very delicious drink and gives strength to delicate people.

Port Wine Flip.—*(Use a large bar glass.)*

1 fresh Egg.
½ table-spoonful of sugar.
¾ glass of shaved ice.
1 wine glass of Port Wine.

Shake well in a shaker, strain into a wine glass, grate a little nutmeg on top, and serve.

Glasgow Flip.—*(Use a large bar glass.)*

Beat 1 Egg thoroughly.
Add the Juice of 1 Lemon.
½ table-spoon powdered sugar.
Balance cold Ginger Ale.
Stir well, and serve.

Gin Flip.—*(Use a large bar glass.)*

1 table-spoon Sugar dissolved in a little Seltzer water.
1 wine glass Holland Gin.

Fill glass half full with fine ice, shake well, and strain into a fancy glass, and serve.

Port Wine Negus.—*(Use a small bar glass.)*

1 tea-spoon Sugar.
1 wine glass Port Wine.
Fill glass ⅓ full of hot water.

Grate a little nutmeg on top, and serve.

Brandy Fix.—*(Use a large bar glass.)*

>   ½ table-spoonful of sugar.
>   2 or 3 dashes of Lime or Lemon Juice.
>   ½ pony glass of Pineapple Syrup.
>   1 or 2 dashes of Chartreuse (green), dissolved well with a
>   little water or Seltzer.
>   Fill up the glass with shaved ice.
>   1 wine glass of Brandy.

Stir up with a spoon, and ornament the top with grapes, and berries in season, and serve with a straw.

Apple Jack Fix.—*(Use a large bar glass.)*

Same as Brandy Fix, using Apple Jack instead.

Gin Fix.—*(Use a large bar glass.)*

>   ½ table-spoonful of sugar.
>   3 or 4 dashes of Lime or Lemon Juice.
>   ½ pony glass of Pineapple Syrup, dissolve well with a
>   little water.
>   Fill up the glass with shaved ice.
>   1 wine glass of Holland Gin..

Stir up well with a spoon, ornament the top with fruit in season, and serve with a straw.

Santa Cruz Fix.

Same as above, substituting Santa Cruz Rum for Gin.

St. Croix Fix.—*(Use a large bar glass.)*

>   Fill glass with fine ice.
>   ½ table-spoon sugar.
>   ½ wine glass Seltzer.
>   2 or 3 dashes Lemon Juice.
>   ½ pony Pineapple Syrup.
>   1 wine glass St. Croix Rum.

Stir well.   Dress with fruit.   Serve with a straw.

St. Croix Fiz.

Same as above, substituting St. Croix Rum for Brandy.

Brandy Fiz.—*(Use a large bar glass.)*

½ tea-spoon fine sugar.
Juice of half a Lemon.
1 wine glass Brandy.
1 or 2 dashes of white of Egg.
¾ glass fine ice. Shake well.
Strain into a fiz glass; fill up with seltzer or vichy.
This must be imbibed immediately.

Gin Fiz.—*(Use a large bar glass.)*

½ table-spoonful sugar.
3 or 4 dashes of Lemon Juice.
½ glass of shaved ice.
1 wine glass of Old Tom Gin.
Stir up well with a spoon, strain it into a large sized bar gla_
fill up the balance with Vichy or Selters water, mix well and
serve.
Bear in mind that all drinks called Fizes, must be drank as
soon as handed out, or the natural taste of the same is lost to
the customer.

Golden Fiz.—*(Use a large bar glass.)*

1 table-spoonful of fine white sugar.
3 dashes of Lemon or Lime Juice.
The yolk of 1 Egg.
1 wine glass of Old Tom Gin.
2 or 3 small lumps of ice.
Shake up thoroughly, strain into a medium bar glass, and fill it
up with Seltzer water.

Morning Glory Fiz.—*(Use a large bar glass.)*

Fill the glass three-quarters full with fine ice.
Mix 3 or 4 dashes Absinthe in a little water.
3 dashes Lime Juice.
4 or 5 dashes Lemon Juice.
1 table-spoon sugar.
The white of 1 Egg.
A wine-glass of Scotch Whiskey.
Shake well in a shaker and strain; fill balance of glass with
Seltzer or Vichy water.
To be drank immediately, or the effect will be lost. It is a
morning beverage, a tonic and a nerve quieter.

Santa Cruz Fiz.—*(Use a medium bar glass.)*

> 1 tea-spoonful of fine white sugar.
> 3 dashes of Lemon Juice.
> 1 small lump of ice.
> 1 wine glass of Santa Cruz Rum.

Fill up the glass with Seltzer water from a syphon, or with Apollinaris water, stir thoroughly, and serve.

Whiskey Fiz.—*(Use a large bar glass.)*

> ½ table-spoonful of sugar.
> 2 or 3 dashes of Lemon Juice, dissolve with a squirt of
>   Seltzer water.
> Fill the glass with ice.
> 1 wine glass of Whiskey.

Stir up well, strain into a good sized fiz glass; fill the balance up with Seltzer or Vichy water, and serve.

This drink must be drank as soon as mixed, in order not to lose its flavor.

Gin and Molasses.—*(Use a whiskey glass.)*

Cover the bottom of the glass with a little gin. Drop in 1 table-spoon of New Orleans molasses, then place the bottle of gin to the customer, allowing him to help himself. After dropping in the molasses, put a small bar spoon in the glass.

Hot water must be used to clean the glass afterwards.

Gin and Calamus.—*(Use a whiskey glass.)*

Steep 2 or 3 pieces calamus root, cut in small bits in a bottle of gin until the essence is extracted.

To serve, you simply hand out the glass together with the bottle, allowing the customer to help himself.

Gin and Pine.

Take some fine slivers of pine wood from the center of a green pine log, steep them in a bottle of gin to extract the flavor; in about two hours the gin will be ready to serve, which is done in same manner as dispensing gin and tansy.

Gin and Tansy.—*(Use a wine glass.)*

Fill a quart decanter one-third full of tansy, and fill up the balance with gin. Serve to customers in a wine glass.

Gin Sling.—*(Use a small bar glass.)*

1 small tea-spoonful of fine white sugar.
1 wine glass of water.
1 wine glass of Gin
1 small lump of ice.

Dissolve the sugar in the water, add the   gin   and ice, stir thoroughly with a spoon. Grate a little nutmeg on top, and serve.

Hot Gin Sling.—*(Use a hot water glass.)*

1 piece of loaf sugar, dissolve in a little water.
1 wine glass of Holland Gin.
Fill up the balance with hot water.

Stir with a spoon, and grate a little nutmeg on top, and serve. Add a slice of lemon if the customer desires it.

Cold Whiskey Sling.—*(Use a small bar glass.)*

1 tea-spoonful of sugar.
½ wine glass of water, dissolve well.
1 or 2 small lumps of ice.
1 wine glass of Whiskey.

Mix well, grate a little nutmeg on top, and serve.

This is an old fashioned drink generally called for by old gentlemen.

Hot Whiskey Sling.—*(Use a medium bar glass, hot.)*

1 small tea-spoonful of powdered sugar.
1 wine glass of Bourbon or Rye Whiskey.

Dissolve the sugar in a little hot water, add the whiskey, and fill the glass two-thirds full of boiling water. Grate a little nutmeg on top, and serve.

Hot Brandy Sling.—*(Use a medium bar glass, hot.)*

1 small tea-spoonful of powdered sugar.
1 wine glass full of Brandy.

Dissolve the sugar in a little boiling water, add the brandy, and fill the glass two-thirds full of boiling water. Grate a little nutmeg on top, and serve.

Brandy Sling.—*(Use a small bar glass.)*

    1 small tea-spoonful of powdered white Sugar.
    1 wine glass of water.
    1 small lump of ice.
    1 wine glass of Brandy.
Dissolve the sugar in the water, add the brandy and ice, stir well with a spoon. Grate a little nutmeg on top, and serve.

Hot Scotch Whiskey Sling.—*(Use a hot water glass.)*

    A wine glass Scotch Whiskey.
    A lump of Sugar.
    A piece of Lemon peel.
Fill glass ¾ full with boiling water; grate nutmeg on top, and serve.

Scotch Whiskey Skin.—*(Use a small bar glass.)*

    1 lump of white Sugar.
    1 small wine glass of Glenlivet, or Islay Whiskey.
    1 small piece of Lemon-rind.
First rinse the glass with hot water, put in the sugar, fill the glass half full of boiling water, add the whiskey and stir. Serve with a spoon.

Irish Whiskey Skin.—*(Use a small bar glass.)*

    1 lump of white Sugar.
    1 small wine glass of Irish Whiskey.
    1 small piece of Lemon peel.
Proceed as directed for Scotch Whiskey Skin.

Brandy Smash.—*(Use a large bar glass.)*

    ½ table-spoon Sugar.
    ½ wine glass water.
    2 or 3 sprigs Mint, pressed as in Mint Julep.
    1 wine glass Brandy.
    Fill glass ½ full fine ice.
Stir well; strain into a fancy bar glass, and serve.

Gin Smash.—*(Use a large bar glass.)*

½ the glass fine ice.
½ table-spoon Sugar.
2 or 3 sprigs Mint, pressed as in Mint Julep.
1 wine glass Holland Gin.

Stir well; strain into a sour glass; dress with fruit; and serve.

Whiskey Smash.—*(Use a small bar glass.)*

1 tea-spoonful of fine white Sugar.
2 tea-spoonfuls of water.
3 or 4 sprigs of young Mint.
1 wine glass of Whiskey.

Hot Apple Toddy.—*(Use a hot apple toddy glass.)*

In mixing this drink, an extra-large hot water glass must be used. Mix as follows:

½ medium-sized well roasted Apple.
½ table-spoonful of Sugar, dissolve well with a little hot water.
1 wine glass full of Old Apple Jack.

Fill the balance with hot water, mix well with a spoon, grate a little nutmeg on top and serve with a bar spoon.

If the customer desires the drink strained, use a fine strainer, such as used for milk punches; attention must be given while roasting the apples that they are not overdone, but done in a nice and juicy manner; use only apples of the finest quality.

Cold Brandy Toddy.—*(Use a whiskey glass.)*

½ tea-spoonful of Sugar.
½ wine glass of water, dissolve well with a spoon:
1 or 2 lumps of broken ice.
1 wine glass of Brandy.

Stir up well, remove the ice, and serve.

It is proper to dissolve the sugar with the water, and hand the bottle of liquor, and glass and spoon to the customer to help himself.

Hot Brandy Toddy.—*(Use a small bar glass, hot.)*

1 tea-spoonful of fine white Sugar.
1 wine glass of Brandy.

Dissolve the sugar in a little boiling water, add the brandy, and pour boiling water into the glass until it is two-thirds full. Grate a little nutmeg on top.

Gin Toddy.—*(Use a whiskey glass.)*

½ tea-spoonful of Sugar, dissolve well in a little water.
1 or 2 lumps of broken ice.
1 wine glass of Holland Gin.
Stir up well and serve.
The proper way to serve this drink, is to dissolve the sugar
with a little water, put the spoon and ice in the glass, and
hand out the bottle of liquor to the customer to help himself.

Hot Gin Toddy.—*(Use a small bar glass, hot.)*

1 tea-spoonful of powdered white Sugar.
1 wine glass of Holland, or Old Tom Gin, as preferred.
Dissolve the sugar in boiling water, add the gin, and pour
boiling water into the glass until it is two-thirds full.

Whiskey Toddy.—*(Use a small bar glass.)*

1 tea-spoon Sugar dissolved in water.
A piece of ice.
1 wine glass Whiskey.
Stir and serve; or dissolve the sugar in the glass with a little
water, and set the bottle of whiskey before the customer.

Hot Whiskey Toddy.

Same as hot Gin Toddy, substituting Whiskey for Gin.

Brandy Daisy.—*(Use a small bar glass.)*

3 or 4 dashes of Gum Syrup.
½ the juice of a Lemon.
2 or 3 dashes Orange Cordial.
1 wine glass Brandy.
Fill glass half full fine ice, shake thoroughly, strain and fill up
with Seltzer water or Apollinaris.

Gin Daisy.

Same as Brandy Daisy, substituting Gin for Brandy.

Ginger Daisy.

Same as above, substituting Jamaica Ginger.

Rum Daisy.

Same as Brandy Daisy, substituting Rum for Brandy.

Brandy and Soda.—*(Use a large bar glass.)*

    1 wine-glass Brandy.
    ½ glass with fine ice.
    Fill up with plain soda.
The above is a pleasing drink for summer.

Brandy and Gum.—*(Use a whiskey glass.)*

    1 or 2 dashes Gum Syrup.
    1 or 2 lumps ice.
Place a spoon in the glass, and hand with a bottle of brandy to the customer.

Egg Nogg.—*(Use a large bar glass.)*

    1 Egg.
    1 table-spoonful of white Sugar.
    1 wine glass Brandy.
    ½ wine glass of Rum (St. Croix or Santa Cruz).
Fill the tumbler ½ full of cracked ice and the balance with milk, shake well together, and grate nutmeg on top, and serve.

Baltimore Egg Nogg.— *(Use a large bar glass.)*

    Take the yellow of one Egg, 1 table-spoonful of Sugar, beat to a Cream, then add some grated Nutmeg, and beat all together, pour in ½ wine glass of Brandy, ½ pony glass St. Croix Rum, 1 wine glass of Madeira Wine, put 2 or 3 lumps of ice into the glass and fill with milk, shake well and grate Nutmeg on top.

Sherry Egg Nogg.—*(Use a large bar glass.)*

    1 Egg.
    1 table-spoonful of Sugar.
    1 pony glass of Brandy.
    1 wine glass of Sherry Wine.
    3 or 4 lumps of ice.
Fill with milk, shake well, and grate nutmeg on top.

Cider Egg Nogg.—*(Use a large bar glass.)*

    1 Egg.
    1 table-spoonful of Sugar.
    Small quantity of cracked ice.
    1 pony glass of Brandy.
Fill the tumbler with Cider, shake well, and serve.

General Harrison Egg Nogg.—*(Use a large bar glass.)*

    3 or 4 small pieces of ice.
    1 fresh Egg.
    1 table-spoon Sugar.
Fill with cider, shake well, and strain; serve with a little nutmeg on top.

Imperial Egg Nogg.—*(Use a large bar glass.)*

    1 table-spoon Sugar.
    1 fresh Egg.
    ⅓ glass of fine ice.
    1 wine glass Brandy.
    ½   "   Jamaica Rum.
Fill up with rich milk. Shake thoroughly in an "egg nogg" shaker, and strain. Grate a little nutmeg on top, if desired.
Hot Egg Nogg—use hot milk and omit the ice.

Egg Nogg for the Bar or a Party.—*(3½ gallons.)*

    20 fresh Eggs.
    2½ quarts fine old Brandy.
    1   pint of Santa Cruz Rum.
    2½ gallons of rich Milk.
    2   pounds of white Sugar.
Separate the whites of the eggs from the yolks, beat each separately with an egg-beater until the yolks are well cut up, and the whites assume a light, fleecy appearance. Mix all the ingredients (except the milk and the whites of the eggs) in a large punch bowl. Then pour in the milk gradually, continually stirring, in order to prevent the milk from curdling with the eggs. Grate sufficient nutmeg on the mixture, and lastly, let the whites float on top, and ornament with colored sugars. Cool in a tub of ice, and serve.

"Arf and Arf," or Black and Tan.—*(Use a large ale glass.)*

This is a common English drink and means half porter and half ale, but in this country we use half old ale and half new.

It is always best to ask the customer how he desires it.

Brandy Straight.—*(Use a small bar glass.)*

Put a piece of ice in the glass, set the bottle on the bar, and allow your customer to help himself.

Pony Brandy.—*(Use a pony glass.)*

Set before the customer a small bar glass, and another containing ice water.

Fill a pony glass with best brandy, and pour it into the empty glass.

Rhine Wine and Seltzer Water.—*(Use a large bar glass.)*

Pour in Rhine Wine until the glass is half full.
Add two small lumps of ice.
Fill the glass with Seltzer water.

Sherry and Bitters.—*(Use a sherry wine glass.)*

1 dash Angostura Bitters.
1 wine glass Sherry.

To prepare the above artistically, dash in your bitters, then twist the glass in a way to cover the inside; fill up with sherry, and serve.

Sherry and Egg.—*(Use a whiskey glass.)*

1 Egg, ice cold.
1 wine glass Sherry Wine.

Before dropping in the egg, cover the bottom of the glass with a little sherry, this will prevent the egg adhering to the glass, or, after preparing the egg as above, set the bottle of sherry before the customer and allow him to help himself.

Sherry and Ice.—*(Use a whiskey glass.)*

1 or 2 lumps of ice and a small bar spoon in the glass, hand this to the customer with the bottle of sherry, allowing him to help himself.

Vermouth Frappe.—*(Use a large bar glass.)*

1½ pony French Vermouth.
½ glass filled with shaved ice.
Fill up with cold Seltzer water.

Knickerbocker.—*(Use a small bar glass.)*

½ a Lime or small Lemon.
3 tea-spoonfuls of Raspberry Syrup.
1 wine glass of Santa Cruz Rum.
3 dashes of Curacoa.

Squeeze out the juice of the lime or lemon into the glass, add the rind and the other materials. Fill the glass one-third full of fine ice, shake up well, and strain into a cocktail glass.

If not sufficiently sweet, add a little more syrup.

Knickerbein.—*(Use a sherry wine glass.)*

⅓ of a wine glass of Vanilla Cordial.
1 yolk of Egg, which carefully cover with Benedictine.
⅓ wine glass of Kümmel.
2 drops Angostura or Boker's Bitters.

The same rule is here applied as in making Poussé Café, viz.: Keep colors separate and the different portions from running into each other.

Brunswick Cooler.—*(Use a large bar glass.)*

Juice of 1 Lemon.
½ table-spoon powdered Sugar.
1 bottle cold Ginger Ale.

Stir well; dress with fruit, and serve.

Rocky Mountain Cooler.

1 Egg beaten up.
½ table-spoon powdered Sugar.
Juice of 1 small Lemon.

Add cider, stir well, grate a little nutmeg on top, if desired.

Peach and Honey.—*(Use a small bar glass.)*

1 table-spoon Honey.
1 wine glass Peach Brandy.

Stir well with a spoon, and serve.

Soda Nectar.—*(Use a large soda glass.)*

The juice of 1 Lemon.
¾ tumbler full of water.
Powdered white Sugar to taste.
2 or 3 small lumps of ice.
½ small tea-spoonful of Carbonate of Soda.

Strain the juice of the lemon, and add it to the water, with sufficient white sugar to sweeten the whole nicely, and stir up until cool. When well mixed, put in the soda, stir well, and drink while the mixture is in an effervescing state.

Family Beer.

10 galls. boiling water.
15 oz. ground Ginger.
10 oz. Cream Tartar.
10 Lemons sliced.

Put all together and when nearly cool strain and add 15 lbs. brown sugar. After which cut ½ oz. oil of cloves and ½ oz. oil cinnamon, in 4 oz. alcohol. When luke-warm, put in 1 pint of yeast and in 15 hours skim and filter it. If bottled, tie corks down carefully.

Saratoga Brace-Up.—*(Use a large bar glass.)*

1 table-spoonful of fine white Sugar.
2 dashes of Angostura Bitters.
4 dashes of Lemon or Lime Juice.
2 dashes of Absinthe.
1 fresh Egg.
1 wine glass of Brandy.
2 or 3 small lumps of ice.

Shake up thoroughly, strain into another glass, and fill it up with seltzer water.

Blue Blazer.—*(Use two silver plated mugs.)*

1 small tea-spoonful of powdered white Sugar dissolved
in 1 wine glass of boiling water.
1 wine glass of Scotch Whiskey.

Put the whiskey and the boiling water in one mug, ignite the liquid with fire, and while blazing mix both ingredients by pouring them four or five times from one mug to the other. If well done this will have the appearance of a continued stream of liquid fire.

Serve in a small bar glass with a piece of twisted lemon peel.

The novice in mixing this beverage should be careful not to scald himself. To become proficient in throwing the liquid from one mug to the other, it will be necessary to practise for some time with cold water.

Currant Shrub.—*(General rule for preparing.)*.

1 quart of strained Current Juice.
1½ pounds of loaf Sugar.

Boil it gently eight or ten minutes, skimming it well; take it off, and when luke-warm, add half a gill of brandy to every pint of shrub. Bottle tight.

A little shrub mixed with ice water makes a delicious drink.

Shrub may be made of cherry or raspberry juice by this method, but the quantity of sugar must be reduced.

Imperial Brandy Punch.—*(For a party of twenty.)*

1 gallon of water.
3 quarts of Brandy.
1 pint of Jamaica Rum.
1½ pounds of white Sugar.
Juice of 6 Lemons.
3 Oranges sliced.
1 Pineapple, pared, and cut up.
1 gill of Curacoa.
2 gills of Raspberry Syrup.
Ice, and add Berries in season.

Mix the materials well together in a large bowl, and you have a splendid punch.

If not sweet enough, add more sugar.

Hot Brandy and Rum Punch.—*(For a party of fifteen.)*

1 quart of Jamaica Rum.
1 quart of Cognac Brandy.
1 pound of white loaf Sugar.
4 Lemons.
3 quarts of boiling water.
1 tea-spoonful of Nutmeg.

Rub the sugar over the lemons until it has absorbed all the yellow part of the skins, then put the sugar into a punch bowl; add the ingredients well together; pour over them the boiling water, stir well together; add the rum, brandy and nutmeg; mix thoroughly, and the punch will be ready to serve.

Tip-Top Brandy.—*(For a party of five.)*

1 bottle of Champagne.
2 bottles of Soda water.
1 liqueur glass of Curacoa.
2 table-spoonfuls of powdered Sugar.
1 slice of Pineapple, cut up.

Put all the ingredients together in a small punch bowl, mix well, ice and serve in champagne goblets.

Oxford Punch.—*(Patronized by the students of Oxford.)*

1 pint of Cognac Brandy.
1 pint of old Jamaica Rum.
1 quart of Orange Shrub.
½ pint of Sherry.
1 bottle of Capillaire.
2 quarts of boiling water.
6 glasses of Calf's Foot Jelly.
6 Lemons.
4 sweet Oranges.
Sufficient loaf Sugar, dissolved in some of the hot water.

Rub the rinds of three lemons with sugar to extract the essential oil. Cut the peel very fine off two more lemons and two of the oranges. Press out the juice of all the oranges and lemons. Place the whole, with the jelly, in a jug and stir well. Pour on the water, and let it stand for twenty minutes. Strain through a fine sieve into a large bowl; add the capillaire, spirits, shrub, and wine, stirring well.

White Plush.—*(Use a small bar glass.)*

Place before the customer a bottle of bourbon or rye whiskey and let him help himself.

Fill up the glass with fresh milk.

The origination of this drink is given by a New York paper to the following effect: A party of dry goods men got hold of a country buyer and proceeded to make matters pleasant for him. They took him to a small bar room and, with the intent to get him full and then work him for a big order, were about to open wine. The countryman, although having indulged in hard cider and whiskey unlimitedly for a number of years, proved not to be so much of a flat as was thought. He pleaded temperance, said he never drank, and guessed he'd take a glass of water, as he was kinder thirsty walkin' round so much. This was rather a set back to his companions. They were assured he had plenty of money to spend, but he was one who required considerable warming up before he would talk the kind of business they desired. "O, take something; take some milk," they said. He replied: "Well, I guess a glass of milk would go sorter good." Some suggested Kumyss, but as there was none in the place they gave him some milk and seltzer, to which, in answer to a wink from some of them, a dash of whiskey was added. He thought the seltzer was what favored it. Next round, seltzer was omitted and more whiskey added. This was continued until he was pretty well set up, and finally got funny and tipped over his glass upon the table. As it spread around he exclaimed: "Gosh, it looks like white plush, don't it?" "So it does," said the boys. "Give the gentleman another yard of white plush!" And it has since been known by that name.

Punch a la Romaine.—*(For a party of fifteen.)*

> 1 bottle of Rum.
> 1 bottle of Wine.
> 10 Lemons.
> 2 sweet Oranges.
> 2 pounds of powdered Sugar.
> 10 Eggs.

Dissolve the sugar in the juice of the lemons and oranges, adding the thin rind of one orange; strain through a sieve into a bowl, and add by degrees the whites of the eggs beaten to a froth. Place the bowl on ice for a while, then stir in briskly the rum and the wine.

Black Stripe.—*(Use a small bar glass.)*

> 1 wine glass of Santa Cruz Rum.
> 1 table-spoonful of Molasses.

This drink can either be made in Summer or Winter; if in the former season, mix in one table-spoonful of water and cool with shaved ice; if in the latter, fill up the tumbler with boiling water. Grate a little nutmeg on top.

Rum Fustian.

> 1 quart of strong Ale.
> 1 pint of Gin.
> 1 bottle of Sherry.
> 12 Eggs.
> 12 large lumps of Sugar.
> 1 stick of Cinnamon.
> 1 Nutmeg, grated.
> 1 Lemon.

Whisk up the yolks of the eggs and add the ale and gin. Put the Sherry into a sauce pan with the cinnamon, nutmeg, sugar, and the rind of the lemon peeled very thin; when the wine boils, pour it upon the ale mixture and drink while hot.

Saratoga Cooler.—*(Use a large bar glass.)*

> 1 tea-spoonful of powdered white Sugar.
> Juice of half a Lemon.
> 1 bottle of Ginger Ale.
> 2 small lumps of ice.

Stir well and remove the ice before serving.

Claret ' up.

1 bottle of Claret.
½ pint of cold water.
1 table-spoonful of powdered Sugar.
1 tea-spoonful of powdered Cinnamon, Cloves and All
    Spice, mixed.
1 small Lemon.

Mix the ingredients well together, adding the thin rind of the
lemon. This is a nice Summer beverage for evening parties.

Porter Cup.

1 bottle of Porter.
1 bottle of Ale.
1 glass of Brandy.
1 dessert-spoonful of Syrup of Ginger.
3 or 4 lumps of Sugar.
½ Nutmeg, grated.
1 tea-spoonful Carbonate of Soda.
1 Cucumber.

Mix the porter and ale in a covered jug; add the brandy, syrup
of ginger and nutmeg; cover it and expose it to the cold for
half an hour before serving.

Claret Cup a la Brunow.—*(For a party of ten.)*

1½ bottle of Claret.
⅓ pint of Curacoa.
½ pint of Sherry.
¼ pint of Brandy.
1 wine glass of Raspberry Ratafia.
1½ Oranges in slices.
½ a Lemon in slices.
1 bottle of Seltzer water.
1½ bottle of Soda water.

Stir all these together with some sprigs of green balm and
borage, and a small piece of cucumber-rind; sweeten with
capillaire or powdered sugar until it ferments; let it stand one
hour, strain and ice it well. Serve in small glasses.

Crimean Cup, a la Wyndham.—*(For a party of five.)*

1 bottle of Champagne.
2 bottles of Soda water.
1 large wine glass of Maraschino.
½ large wine glass of Cognac.
½ large wine glass of Curacoa.
1 table spoonful of crushed Sugar.

Macerate the thinly peeled rind of half an orange with the sugar; add the Maraschino, Cognac, and Curacoa. Mix thoroughly and add the soda water and Champagne. The addition of half a pound of pure ice is a great improvement.

English Curacoa.

6 ounces of very thin Orange peel.
1 pint of Whiskey.
1 pint of clarified Syrup.
1 drachm powdered Alum.
1 drachm Carbonate of Potash.

Place the orange peel in a bottle, which will hold a quart with the whiskey; cork tightly and let the contents remain for 10 to 12 days, shaking the bottle frequently. Then strain out the peel, add the syrup; shake well, and let it stand for 3 days. Take out a tea-cupful into a mortar, and beat up with the alum and potash; when well mixed, pour it back into the bottle, and let it remain for a week. The Curacoa will then be perfectly clear and equal in flavor to the best imported article.

To Make Blackberry Brandy.

To 10½ gallons pure spirits add :
12 quarts of Blackberries.
4 gallons of water.
6 pounds of loaf Sugar.
¼ ounce of whole Cloves.
½ ounce whole Cinnamon.

Let it stand 21 days, draw off, strain and clarify (clear) if necessary.

Raspberry Brandy.

To 10 gallons of pure proof spirits add :
13 quarts of Raspberries.
2¼ gallons of water.
6 pounds of loaf Sugar.
½ ounce whole Cloves.
½ ounce whole Cinnamon.

Let it stand 21 days, draw off, strain and clarify if necessary.

Peach Brandy.

To 10½ gallons Pure Proof Spirit add:
3½ gallons good Peach Brandy.
2 pounds loaf Sugar.
¼ drachm essential oil of Bitter Almonds, cut in Alcohol.
¼ pint of Orange flower water.
Color it, and let it stand for 7 days; it will then be ready for use.

Cherry Brandy.

To 10½ gallons Pure Proof Spirit add:
12½ quarts bruised Wild Cherries.
After allowing to stand 5 to 7 days, strain it, and add:
6½ pounds loaf Sugar.
2¼ gallons water (fresh spring water if possible).
Then let the whole stand 9 days, draw off, and clarify if required.

Lemon Brandy.

To 10½ gallons Pure Proof Spirit add:
7½ Lemons, sliced.
6½ pounds loaf Sugar.
¼ pound Lemon peel.
1 pint good clear Brandy.
Let it stand 12 days and draw off.

Orange Brandy.

To 10½ gallons Pure Proof Spirit add:
9 Oranges, sliced.
6½ pounds of loaf Sugar.
1 pint Brandy.
½ ounce Tartaric Acid.
Let it stand for 9 days and draw off.

Pineapple Brandy.

To 10½ gallons Pure Proof Spirit add:
4½ Pineapples, sliced.
3 pints simple Syrup (Sugar and water).
1 pint good Brandy.
½ ounce Cassia.
½ ounce Tincture of Saffron.
2¼ gallons water.
Let it stand 12 days, it will then be ready for drawing off and use.

Ginger Brandy.

To 10½ gallons Pure Proof Spirit add :
    ½ ounce Tincture Cardamom Seed.
Take ¼ pound bruised ginger root, digested in ¼ gallon strong
alcohol for 7 days. Add the liquor, after having been filtered
to the pure spirit, agitating it thoroughly, then add :
    2½ gallons pure soft water.
    ½ gallon simple Syrup.
Color with sugar coloring, ready for use. If more flavor is required, use more of the ginger ; if sweeter, more syrup.

Lavender Brandy.

To 10½ gallons Pure Proof Spirit, add :
    1 dr. Oil of Lavender, dissolved for 12 or 13 hours in
        strong Alcohol.
    3 gallons pure soft water.
    ½ ounce Tincture Cinnamon.
    ½ gallon simple Syrup.
Color with sugar, adding more lavender or syrup, if more flavor
or sweetness is required.

Grunswald Brandy.

    1 lb. Orange Peel.
    1 " Centaurium.
    4 oz. Wormwood.
    4 " ground Ginger.
    5 " Calamus Root.
    2 " Trefoil.
    5 " Oil Cloves.
    5 " Cinnamon.
    3 " Oil of Peppermint.
    5 " galls. Alcohol, 95 per cent.
Steep the above in the alcohol for ten days ; strain and add :
    3 qts. white Syrup.
    5 galls. water.
Color with Caramel or burned Sugar.

Carraway Brandy.

Steep 1 oz. of caraway seed, bruised, in 1 pint of brandy. In
one week strain. Add 6 ounces of loaf sugar.

Currant Brandy.

Take 1 quart of black or red currants, and fill up with 1 quart of brandy. In two months strain, and add sugar to taste.

Juniper Berry.

Dissolve ½ drachm oil of juniper in 1 quart of pure spirit or brandy. Add ½ lb. of sugar, dissolve in 1 quart of water.

Usquebaugh.

     1 drachm Oil of Aniseed.
     1 drachm Oil of Cloves.
     1 drachm Essential Oil of Nutmegs.
     20 drops Oil of Cinnamon.
     30 drops Oil of Juniper.

Mix all the oils together, shaking well occasionally for a day or so; then dissolve them in rectified spirits (60 O. P.) one pint; colored with burned sugar, one ounce, and add of each, syrup and boiling water, twelve pints. Mix all together thoroughly and fine with alum, etc.

Rum Shrub.

     ½ gallon bitter Orange Juice.
     8 lbs. refined Sugar.
     1½ gallons Rum, reduced to 40 U. P.

Dissolve the sugar in the juice by aid of a gentle heat, mix this and the rum together, shake up well and set aside to clear. If not bright in a fortnight fine down with isinglass.

Ginger.

Bruise half a pound of the best new Jamaica ginger in an iron mortar, and put it into a bottle containing one pint of spirit of wine (60 O. P.), and one pint of water, allow it to macerate for ten or twelve days, shaking it up well each morning. After the twelfth day transfer it to a funnel containing a paper filter; when all the liquid has run through pass two pints of sherry over it, and lastly, one pint of boiling water. This will yield rather better than half a gallon of liquid. When all are mixed, dissolve in this one ounce of burned sugar, and having added twelve pints of syrup, shake the whole well up, and fine with alum, etc.

Reduced Gin.

To 10½ gallons Pure Proof Spirit, add:
    5 gallons pure Holland Gin.
    3 gills simple Syrup.
Then mix well together.

OR IN THIS MANNER:

To 10½ gallons Pure Spirit, add:
    2½ gallons pure Holland Gin.
    1 pint Syrup.
    1 drachm Oil of Turpentine, cut and mixed in ½ pint
        Alcohol.
    ½ oz. Spirits of Nitre.
Mix well together and it will be ready for use.

Swampscott Jamaica Rum (Imitation).

To 10½ gallons Pure Spirits, add:
    1½ gallons Jamaica (genuine).
    ½ ounce Tincture of Kino.
    1¼ pound loaf Sugar.
    ¾ ounce Butyric Acid, cut or mixed first in Alcohol, and
        left standing thirteen hours, then add to the spirits.
    ½ drachm Caraway Seed Oil.
    ½ drachm Fennel Seed Oil, cut or mixed in ½ pint Alco-
        hol and add after standing fourteen hours.
Mix the whole together and let stand for six days, after
coloring with sugar coloring.

Simple Syrup.

Take 2 pounds of loaf sugar to 1 pint of water, dissolve it
over the fire, remove the scum that arises, as soon as it com-
mences to boil, remove it from the fire, strain it while hot.

Gum Syrup.

Dissolve 2 pounds of loaf sugar and 1 pound of white gum
arabic in 1 quart of hot water, boil over the fire for 2 minutes.

Raspberry Syrup.

Take 1 pint of filtered raspberry juice, mash the raspberries in a pan and let them stand 2 or 3 days until fermentation has commenced, filter the juice through blotting paper, and add 2 pounds of fine sugar. Place the syrup on the fire and as it heats, skim carefully, but do not allow it to boil; when it becomes of a proper consistency, remove it and allow it to cool, then bottle it.

Strawberry Syrup.

Take 4 quarts of strawberries, express the juice and strain, add water until it measures 4 pints, add 8 pounds of powdered sugar, keep it on the fire until it boils, then strain, allow it to cool and bottle.

Lemon Syrup.

1 pint of lemon juice, dissolve 5 pounds of sugar in the lemon juice, add the rinds of 5 lemons, boil for 2 minutes, skim, then strain.

Orgeat Syrup.

Cover with boiling water 2 pounds of sweet almonds, ½ lbs. of bitter almonds, let them stand until cool and then peel them, beat them in a mortar to a fine paste, adding water slowly, press through a linen cloth and dissolve in the liquid 15 pounds of sugar, boil for 2 minutes, then strain.

Cordial Syrup.

35 lbs. refined lump Sugar.
3 gallons boiling water.
Dissolve the sugar in the water and stir in through flannel.

Banana Syrup.

1 gallon white Syrup.
1 oz. Essence of Banana.
A few drops Lemon Extract.

Clove Syrup.

30 drops of Quintessence of Cloves.
1 lb. simple Syrup.
Mix by shaking well together in a bottle.

Ginger Syrup.

> 1 gallon white syrup.
> 12 ounces Tincture of Ginger.

Strain if cloudy.

ANOTHER:

Put 2 ounces Jamaica Ginger into a quart of boiling water, let it remain 24 hours, closely covered, strain, and add 3 pounds crusted sugar; boil to a syrup.

Orange Syrup.

> 2 oz. Tincture of Orange Peel.
> 1 lb. simple Syrup.

Mix.

Pineapple Syrup.

Add 1 ounce essence of Pineapple to 1 gallon white Syrup and half ounce Tartaric Acid.

Sarsaparilla Syrup.

> 10 drops Oil of Anise.
> 20 drops Oil of Winter Green.
> 20 drops Oil of Sassafras.
> 6 ounces of Caramel.
> Cut the Oils in 4 ounces of Alcohol.

Vanilla Syrup.

> 1 gallon white Syrup.
> ½ ounce extract Vanilla.

Wild Cherry Syrup.

4 ounces Wild Cherry Bark, steeped in a pint of cold water 36 hours; press out, and add half pound Sugar, strain.

Aniseed Cordial.

To 15 gallons of pure rectified Whiskey add 2½ drachms of Oil of Aniseed cut in Alcohol, 10 gallons of soft clear water, 4 gallons of simple Syrup; mix well together, and let it lie from 10 to 12 days, it will be then ready for use.

Cinnamon Cordial.

To 12 gallons of pure rectified Whiskey add 4 drachms of Oil of Cinnamon cut in Alcohol, 6 gallons of clear soft water, and 3 gallons of simple Syrup, mix well and let stand for about 12 days.

Strawberry Cordial.

Take 15 gallons of pure rectified Whiskey and add 24 quarts of fresh Strawberries, let stand about 10 days, then draw off and add 9 gallons of pure soft water, and 6 gallons of simple Syrup, let it lie from 10 to 12 days, when it will be ready for use.

Citron Cordial.

- To 15 gallons of pure rectified Whiskey add 5 pounds of Lemon rinds, 3 pounds of Orange peel, 2½ ounces of broken Nutmeg, and let it lie for about 12 days, then add 7½ gallons of soft water, and 4 gallons of simple Syrup, let stand about 10 days, it will then be ready to draw off.

Clove Cordial.

To 3 gallons of pure rectified Whiskey, add ½ drachm Oil of Cloves cut in Alcohol, 1½ gallons of water, 1 gallon of simple Syrup, mix well and let stand 12 days.

Orange Cordial.

To 10 gallons of pure rectified Whiskey, add 1 pound of fresh Lemon peel, 4 pounds of dried Orange peel, and 6 pounds of fresh Orange peel, let it lie for 12 days, then draw it off and add 6 gallons of clear soft water, 3 gallons of simple Syrup, let stand for 10 days, it will then be ready for use.

Rose Cordial.

To 3 gallons of pure rectified Whiskey, add 30 drops of Oil of Roses cut in ½ pint of Alcohol, 2 gallons of pure soft water, and 3 quarts of simple Syrup, mix well together, let stand for 12 days and then draw off ready for use.

Peppermint Cordial.

Boil 12 pounds brown Sugar in 2 gallons of water, add 1½ ounces of Alum and remove the scum as long as it rises, then add ½ ounce of Oil of Peppermint, 5 gallons of pure Spirits, 7 gallons of pure soft water, mix well by stirring and let it stand 24 hours, when it will be ready for use.

Wintergreen Cordial.

To 3 gallons of pure rectified Whiskey add 30 drops of Oil of Wintergreen, cut in ½ pint of Alcohol, 2 gallons of water and 3 quarts of simple Syrup, mix well together, let stand for 12 days, and then draw off ready for use.

Carraway Cordial.

¼ oz. English Oil of Carraway.
3½ pints of Spirit of Wine (60 O. P.)
13 pints Cordial Spirit.
Dissolve the oil in the spirit as above, add the syrup, and if necessary fine with alum and tartar.

Capillaire.

20 lbs. best lump Sugar.
10 pints water.
1 drachm Acetic Acid, strong.
Boil the sugar in the water till it is all dissolved; add the acetic acid, and allow it to remain ten or fifteen minutes on the fire; remove and allow it to cool; then decant; clear into a bottle or jar.

Maraschino Cordial.

3½ gallons 95 per cent. Spirits.
7 gallons white Syrup.
1 gallon Peach Juice.
Filter through canton flannel; bottle for use.

Ginger Gin.

Take of best Jamaica Ginger, bruised small, half a pound; boil it in one gallon of water, and strain through fine muslin. In this dissolve ten pounds of refined Sugar by means of a gentle heat. Over the bruised Ginger which remains in the muslin strainer, pass one gallon unmixed Gin (O. P.), mix this and the Syrup of Ginger together, add finings, and set aside to clear.

Raspberry Cordial.

8 oz. essence of Raspberry.
2½ pints Spirit of Wine (53 O. P.).
13 pints cordial Syrup.
2 oz. Tincture of Cudbear, strong.

Let all these be shaken well up together in a jar, using no
finings, for if the materials are genuine, the cordial will be
bright and ready for use the day it is mixed.

Lemon Cordial.

3 drops essential Oil of Lemon.
3 pints Lemon Juice.
6 oz. Lemon peel, fresh.
6 lbs. refined Sugar.
2 pints rectified Spirit.

Add the oil to the juice, and in it boil the peel, which should be
cut very small, and strain; add to the strained liquor the
sugar; dissolve by aid of gentle heat, and when cool, mix in the
spirit by brisk agitation.

Curacoa Cordial.

1 lb. Orange peel.
¼ lb. ground Cinnamon.
16 Oranges.
6 galls. white Syrup.
Boil 5 minutes.

Add 3 galls. pure spirits, 95 per cent. above; filter through
Canton flannel and bottle.

Lemon Extract.

1 oz. Oil of Lemon.
48 oz. Citric Acid (tincture).
6 gallons Gum Syrup.
Enough water to make 24 gallons.

Before mixing cut the oil in a pint of alcohol.
Filter carefully through charcoal.

Blackberry Extract.

Mash nice blackberries; strain through flannel; to 1 pint of
juice add:

1 lb. crushed Sugar.
½ oz. ground Cinnamon.
¼ oz. Mace.
2 table-spoonfuls powdered Sugar.

Strain; and if desired, add ¼ gill of brandy.

Cider.

When you bottle Cider in warm weather, do not cork it immediately, but let it stand 2 or 3 days, so that it may become flat.

If the cider should happen to be too flat when you are about to bottle it, put a small lump of rock candy and four or five raisins in each bottle, but do not do this unless you are going to use it shortly.

Cider should be well corked and waxed, and stood upright in a cool place.

To fine and improve the flavor of 1 hogshead, take:

    1 gallon of good Brandy.
    ½ ounce of Cochineal.
    1 pound of Alum.
    3 pounds of Rock Candy.

Bruise them well in a mortar and add them to the brandy, letting stand for two days; then mix the whole with the cider, and bung up the cask tightly and let remain for about six months; if fine enough then bottle it.

Cheap Cider from Raisins.

Take seven pounds of raisins and wash them well in four or five waters, until perfectly clean, then put them into a cask with the head out, and pour three gallons of water on them; after which cover up well and let stand for 8 days. At the end of that time rack the liquid off into another cask, let it stand for about five days, when it will be ready for use.

To Keep Cider Good.

Take the cider when you think it will suit your taste, put it into a clean kettle, then take ¼ of a pound of hops, put them in a bag and tie them to the handle of the kettle so as they will hang down inside, but not touch the bottom of the kettle. Put the cider on the fire and let it boil a short time, scumming it whilst boiling; then let it cool and pour it into a cask, adding 1 pint of fresh brandy. Bung up tightly. This cider, so prepared, will keep for years.

Prepared Cider for Imitating Wines.

Take the cider when it suits your taste, and put it into a good strong barrel, and add 3 gallons of Apple Whiskey and a small quantity of mustard seeds; bung up tight and let ferment. In a day or so bore a gimlet hole in the bung, and put a spile into it, so as you can let some of the gas out, so as to prevent the barrel bursting. When fermentation is done, draw off, and clean out the barrel, then put the cider in again, and bung it up close.

Sugar Coloring.

Take 4 pounds of brown sugar, boil it well and burn it so that it will taste bitter, thin it with water while on the fire, pouring in but a little at a time, and keep stirring all the time. If you pour too much in at a time, it will explode, and may burn you. After you have thinned it down to its proper consistency, strain it while warm.

Cooling Wines.

Always ice white wines in summer, if the weather be hot; but with red wines this must not be regarded, as a great degree of cold is apt to affect their flavor. If your cellar be of the requisite degree of coldness, say 52° and the thermometer stand at 70°, the wine is full cold enough to be grateful; and, brought directly from the cellar to the guest, (which it should always be at that season,) the outside of the bottle will be clouded, a sure test that the wine is sufficiently cold. Where ice is not obtainable the bottle may be hung up in a flannel bag, previously soaked in water in the full glare of the sun's rays, where there is also a strong draft of air. The constant evaporation keeping the bag dripping wet, will cool the wine almost to the freezing point. The water of a covered well or spring, drawn fresh, in which a pound or two of salt is thrown, placed in a cool cellar, will reduce the temperature of wine to a very low and agreeable point.

Essence of Lemon.

1 oz. Oil of Lemon.
1 quart Alcohol (95 per cent.).
½ pint water.
1½ oz. Citric Acid.

Grind the citric acid to a powder in a porcelain mortar; dissolve it in the water. Then cut the oil of lemon in the alcohol and add the acid water.

Solferino Coloring.

1 oz. Solferino.
1 pint water.
Put them in a bottle, shake well, and in twenty-four hours it
will be ready for use.

Essence of Cognac.

1 oz. Oil of Cognac.
½ gallon of Spirits (95 per cent.)
1 gallon of Spirits (70 per cent.)
2 oz. strong Ammonia.
1 pound of fine black Tea.
2 pounds of Prunes.
Dissolve the oil of cognac in the 95 per cent. spirits; cork it
tightly in a bottle and let it stand three days, frequently shaking it, then add the ammonia.
Mash the prunes (breaking the kernels) and put them with
the tea and the 70 per cent. spirits into a stone jar of 3 gallons
capacity; cover closely, and let it stand for 8 days.
Filter the liquor, and add it to the solution of oil and
ammonia. Bottle for use.
This quantity is sufficient for flavoring 100 gallons of brandy.

Caramel.

7 pounds of loaf Sugar.
1 pint of water.
Crush and dissolve the sugar in the water; boil it in a 5 gallon
copper kettle, stirring occasionally, until it gets brown; when
it begins to burn, reduce the fire; let it burn until the smoke
becomes offensive to the eyes; then try it by dipping a rod into
it, and letting a few drops fall into a glass of cold water; if it
settles at the bottom and crystallizes, so that it will crack, it is
done. Then take about half gallon luke-warm water, and pour
it in by degrees, stirring all the time. When thoroughly mixed,
filter it while hot through a coarse flannel filter.

Tincture of Orange Peel.

1 pound of dried Orange peel (ground).
1 gallon of Spirits (95 per cent).
Place them in a closely corked vessel for 10 days.
Strain and bottle for use.

Tincture of Lemon Peel.

Cut into small chips the peel of 12 large lemons. Place it in a glass jar and pour over it 1 gallon spirits, 70 per cent. Let it stand until the lemon peel has all sunk to the bottom of the liquor. It is then ready for use without either filtering or straining.

Tincture of Cloves.

Take 1 pound of ground cloves; warm them over a fire until quite hot; put them quickly into a jar, pour on them 1 gallon 95 per cent. alcohol, cover them air-tight, and let them stand for 10 days. Draw off into bottles and cork close.

Tincture of Cinnamon.

Place 2 pounds of ground cinnamon into a jar with 1 gallon 95 per cent. alcohol, closely covered. At the end of 8 days strain the liquor clear; wash the sediment with 1 quart proof spirits; strain it; mix the two liquors together, and filter through blotting paper.

Tincture of Allspice and Tincture of Gentian.

Prepared same as above, substituting allspice and gentian for cinnamon.

Aromatic Tincture.

1 ounce of Ginger.
1 ounce of Cinnamon.
1 ounce of Orange peel.
½ ounce of Valerian.
2 quarts of Alcohol.

Macerate the ingredients in the alcohol in a close vessel for fourteen days, then filter through filtering paper. This is sometimes employed to give a flavor to milk punch, but it must be used with precaution. Ten drops are sufficient for a pint of punch.

Angostura Bitters.

    4 oz. Angostura Bark.
    1 oz. Chamomile Flowers.
    ¼ oz. Cardamom Seeds.
    ¼ oz. Cinnamon Bark.
    1 oz. Orange peel.
    1 lb. Raisins.
    2½ gallons Proof Spirit.
Macerate for a month, then press and filter.

Orange Bitters.

    1½ lbs. freshly dried Orange peel.
    1½ oz. Coriander Seeds.
    1½ drachm Carraway Seeds.
    1½ drachm Cardamom Seeds.
    6 pints rectified Spirits (60 O. P.).
    3 oz. burned Sugar.
    7 pints Syrup.
    Water, sufficient to make up two gallons.
Steep the seeds and peel in the spirit for fourteen or twenty
days, when it must be drained off and replaced by water; which
after two days drain off and replace by a second quantity of
water.   Let the three tinctures thus obtained be mixed
together, and first the coloring and then the syrup be added.
This, if allowed to remain a short time undisturbed, will become bright; or if wanted for immediate use, may be filtered
through fine linen.

Wormwood Bitters.

    2 drops oil of Lemon.
    2 drops oil of Carraway.
    2 drops oil of Absinthe.
    2 oz. extract of Licorice.
    ½ oz. extract Chamomile.
    3 pints rectified Spirit (60 O. P.).
    3 pints Syrup.
    Water, enough to make two gallons.
Dissolve the oils in the spirit, and extracts in water, add both
together at once, shake violently for some minutes; next add
the syrup and the remainder of the water, and again shake well
up.   Let it stand aside some days, the longer the better, then
filter through paper.

Wine Bitters.

>1 thin peel of Lemon.
>1 thin peel of bitter Orange.
>3 oz. good Sherry.
>2 oz. water.

Infuse.

Stoughton Bitters.

Mix together the following ingredients, and let stand for 5 weeks. Gentian, 4 ounces, Orange peel, 4 ounces, Columbo, 4 ounces, Camomile Flowers, 4 ounces, Quassia, 4 ounces, burnt Sugar, 1 pound, Whiskey, 2½ gallons. Bottle the clear liquor.

Essence of Bitters.

>½ lb. dried Orange peel.
>¼ lb. Orange Apples.
>½ lb. Gentian Root.
>¼ lb. Lemon peel, ground to powder.

Macerate for ten days. Add one gallon of pure spirit. Strain and add one quart of soft water.

"Pick-Me-Up" Bitters.

>1 oz. Angostura Bark.
>1 oz. Orange Peel.
>1 oz. Lemon Peel.
>1 oz. Chireta.
>½ oz. Chamomile Flowers.
>¼ oz. Cinnamon Bark.
>¼ oz. Cardamom Seeds.
>¼ oz. Carraway Seeds.
>4 lbs. Raisins.
>1½ gallons Spirits (11 U. P.).

Macerate for a month, then press and filter.

Rum Bitters.

>1 lb. Raisins.
>3 oz. bruised Cinnamon.
>1 oz. Virginia Snake Root.
>Juice of 1 Orange and 1 Lemon.
>20 Cloves.
>Digest in Rum for 2 months.

Brandy Bitters.

> 4 lbs. Gentian Root.
> 2 lbs. Cardamom Seeds.
> 1 lb. Cinnamon Bark.
> ¼ lb. Cochineal.
> 2 lbs. Chireta.

Bruise all these together to the size of barley corns; then add two gallons of brandy. Macerate for about a month, then press out all the liquid; to the residue add one gallon more brandy (some use plain spirit), and after having allowed it to stand one day, press as before; add the two liquids and filter, when it will be ready for use.

Dutch Bitters.

> 2 oz. Wormwood.
> 1 oz. Chamomile Flowers.
> 1 oz. Gentian Root.
> 2 oz. Orange Peel.
> ½ oz. powdered Cloves.
> ¼ oz. Carraway Seeds.
> ½ gallon Capillaire.
> 2 gallons Proof Spirit.

Macerate for a month, then press and filter.

Quinine Bitters.

> 160 grains Sulphate of Quinine.
> 1 lb. Orange Peel, cut small.
> 2 gallons Cape Wine.
> 1 pt. Proof Spirit.

Dissolve the quinine in the spirit by aid of a gentle heat, and pour it over the orange peel. After it has been allowed to remain undisturbed in a close vessel for two days add the wine, and stir up well every day for a fortnight, then press and filter.

Anisette.

> 10 oz. powdered Aniseed.
> 1 oz. powdered Cummin Seed.
> 1 oz. powdered Orris Root.
> 3 oz. Lemon Peel.
> 2 gallons Spirit (30 U. P).
> 3 pts. Capillaire.

Macerate the powders and the peel in spirit for about a month, then filter and add the capillaire.

Aqua Bianca.

¼ oz. Essence of Lemon.
¼ oz. Essence of Citron.
¼ oz. Essence of Amber.
¼ oz. Essence of Peppermint.
¼ oz. Essence of Bergamot.
½ oz. Essence of Rose.
2 gallons Proof Spirit.
5 pints Capillaire.

Mix all together; shake frequently and in one month filter through flannel.

Cordiale de Caladon.

½ lb. Lemon Peel, cut small.
½ oz. Fennel Seed, in coarse powder.
¼ oz. Cardamoms.
1 drachm Aniseed.
1 drachm Cloves.
2 gallons Proof Spirit.
4 pints Capillaire.

Macerate the peel and the powders in the spirit for fourteen days, then press and filter, and add the capillaire.

Citron.

12 oz. Lemon Peel.
1 oz. Essence of Saffron.
2 gallons Proof Spirit.
½ gallon Capillaire.

Macerate the peel in the spirit for fourteen days, then add the essence of saffron and capillaire.

Citronette.

2¼ gallons of Proof Spirit.
¼ gallon Orange Flower Water.
½ gallon Syrup.
10 oz. Lemon Peel.
1½ oz. Essence of Saffron.
¼ oz. Essence of Amber.
¼ oz. Essence of Orange.
1 drachm Essence of Bergamot.

Mix altogether, and in one month press and filter. This is greatly improved by age.

Eau d'Absinthe.

  33 oz. Wormwood.
  24 oz. refined Sugar.
  4 oz. Juniper Berries.
  ¼ oz. Angelica Root.
  1 oz. Cinnamon Bark.
  4 oz. Orange Flower Water.
  2½ gallons Spirit of Wine (11 U. P.).

Bruise the sugar, berries, wormwood, etc., in an iron mortar and place them in a wide mouthed jar; then add the orange water and spirit. Stir them well each day for a month, then press and filter.

Curacoa.

  6 oz. Orange Peel, cut small.
  1 drachm Cinnamon.
  ½ drachm Mace, bruised.
  1 drachm Saffron.
  1¼ gallons Spirit of Wine (14 U. P.).
  2 pints Capillaire.

Macerate all together; in about twenty-one days draw off the liquor through a strainer, and press the residue so as to recover any of the liquor it may have retained; mix both liquors, and filter through flannel.

Eau d'Amis.

  4 oz. Figs.
  4 oz. Raisins.
  4 oz. Dates.
  1 oz. Essence of Saffron.
  6 drops Essence of Bergamot.
  10 drops Essence of Citron.
  1½ gallons Proof Spirit.
  10 lbs. brown Sugar.
  6 pints distilled water.

Beat up the figs, dates, etc., with a part of the sugar until they form a paste; place this in a wide mouthed jar, and having previously mixed together the liquids, add a quart at a time, stirring well between each addition. Then add the balance of the sugar, and in one month press and filter.

Eau de Cordiale.

20 oz. Lemon Peel.
4 oz. Cinnamon Bark, bruised.
2 oz. Balm, the fresh herb.
2 oz. powdered Coriander Seed.
2 oz. powdered Aniseed.
1 oz. powdered Mace.
1 oz. powdered Nutmeg.
2½ gallons rectified Spirit (60 O. P.).
2 gallons distilled water.
1 gallon Capillaire.

Macerate the solids for ten days in the spirits, and decant as much liquor as can be got off clear. To the mace add the water and capillaire; stir well up and set aside for fourteen days; then press, filter and add the liquor first withdrawn. Another method, and it is thought a better one, is to mix all the ingredients together, and stir them well up every other morning for about a month, and then to press and filter.

Brandy Cocktail for Bottling.

5 gallons of Spirits (70 per cent.)
2 gallons of water.
1 quart Gum Syrup.
¼ pint Essence of Cognac.
1 oz. Tincture of Cloves.
1 ounce Tincture of Gentian.
2 ounces Tincture of Orange Peel.
¼ ounce Tincture of Cardamoms.
½ ounce Tincture of Licorice Root.

Mix the essence and tinctures with a portion of the spirits. Add the remainder of the ingredients and color with a sufficient quantity of solferino and caramel, equal parts, to give the desired color.

Gin Cocktail for Bottling.

5 gallons of Gin.
2 gallons of water.
1 quart of Gum Syrup.
2 ounces of Tincture of Orange Peel.
7 ounces of Tincture of Gentian.
½ ounce of Tincture of Cardamoms.
½ ounce of Tincture of Lemon Peel.

Mix them together, and give the desired color with solferino and caramel, in equal proportions.

Bourbon Cocktail for Bottling.

5 gallons of Bourbon.
2 gallons of water.
1 quart of Gum Syrup.
2 ounces of Tincture of Orange Peel.
1 ounce of Tincture of Lemon Peel.
1 ounce of Tincture of Gentian.
½ ounce of Tincture of Cardamoms.

Mix these ingredients thoroughly, and color with solferino and caramel, in equal proportions.

Essence of Claret Wine Punch for Bottling.

5 gallons of Claret Wine.
2½ gallons of Spirits (70 per cent.).
3 gallons of plain Syrup.
1 pint of Tincture of Lemon peel.
½ pint of Raspberry Juice.
1 ounce of Tartaric Acid.
1½ ounce of Tincture of Coves.
1½ ounce of Tincture of Cinnamon.

First dissolve the tartaric acid in a small portion of the spirits. Mix the tinctures with the remainder of the spirits. Pour the two mixtures together, and add the remaining ingredients.

Essence of Regent Punch for Bottling.

1 gallon of pure Cognac.
1 gallon of pure Jamaica Rum.
6 pounds of loaf Sugar.
3 gallons of water.
1 ounce of green Tea.
30 Lemons.
7 Oranges.
9 drachms of ground Cinnamon.
⅓ drachm of ground Cloves.
1 drachm of ground Vanilla.

Macerate the peel of 7 lemons and 7 oranges in the cognac and rum for 24 hours. Boil the sugar in the water; skim and add the tea. When cool, mix with the liquor and add the juice of the 30 lemons and 7 oranges. Filter and bottle for use.

Duke of Norfolk Punch for Bottling.

 20 quarts of French Brandy.
 30 Lemons.
 30 Oranges.
 30 quarts of cold boiled water.
 15 pounds of double-refined Sugar.
 2 quarts of new Milk.

Pare off the peel of the oranges and lemons very thin, excluding all of the white rind. Infuse in the brandy for twelve hours. Dissolve the sugar in the water; add the juice of the oranges and of twenty-four of the lemons; pour this upon the brandy and peels, mixing thoroughly. Strain through a very fine hair sieve into a barrel that has held spirits, and add the milk. Stir and bung close. After it has stood six weeks in a warm cellar, bottle, in perfectly clean and dry bottles, well corked. This will keep for years and improve with age.

Essence of Arrack Punch for Bottling.

 1½ gallons Batavia Arrack.
 3 gallons Spirits (70 per cent.)
 3 gallons plain Syrup.
 ½ pint of Tincture Lemon peel.

Mix together. Ready for immediate use.

Essence of Wine Punch for Bottling.

 5 gallons Port or Marseilles Wine.
 1½ gallons Spirits (70 per cent.)
 3 gallons plain Syrup.
 3 ounces Tartaric Acid.
 3 ounces Tincture of Allspice.

Dissolve the tartaric acid in a portion of the spirits. Mix that with the remainder of the spirits and add the other ingredients.

Essence of Bourbon Whiskey Punch.

 4½ gallons Bourbon Whiskey.
 3 gallons plain Syrup.
 ½ pint Tincture of Lemon peel.
 ¼ pint Tincture of Orange peel.
 3 oz. Tincture of Allspice.
 5 dessert-spoonsful Tincture of Cloves.

Mix the Tinctures thoroughly with the whiskey, and add the syrup.

 The essence of Rum Punch may be made by substituting Jamaica or Santa Cruz rum for whiskey.

Empire City Punch for Bottling.

> 5 oz. sweet Almonds.
> 5 oz. bitter Almonds.
> 1 oz. powdered Cinnamon.
> ½ oz. powdered Cloves.
> 5 oz. plain Syrup.
> 2 gallons Bourbon Whiskey.
> 1 gallon Raspberry Syrup.
> 7 gallons of water.

Scald the almonds and peel them, wash them, rub them well with the plain syrup and spices. Boil the whole about five minutes in the water, and when cool, strain through a plain flannel filter. Then add the whiskey and raspberry syrup, mixing all together thoroughly.

Imperial Raspberry Whiskey Punch for Bottling.

> 2 gallons Whiskey.
> 1 gallon Raspberry Syrup.
> 7 gallons water.
> 5 oz. plain Syrup.
> 5 oz. sweet Almonds.
> 5 oz. bitter Almonds.
> 1¼ oz. of powdered Cinnamon.
> ⅛ oz. of powdered Cloves.

Bruise and infuse the almonds in sufficient boiling water; skim and add the cinnamon, cloves and syrup; rub them fine, and boil them for five minutes in the seven gallons of water; strain, and, when cool, add the whiskey and raspberry syrup.

Essence of St. Domingo Punch for Bottling.

> 10 gallons of Arrack.
> 6 gallons of plain Syrup.
> 2 ounces of Tartaric Acid.
> 5 drops of Oil of Cloves.
> 10 drops of Oil of Lemon.
> 5 drops of Oil of Orange.
> 5 drops of Oil of Cinnamon.
> 2 ounces of Alcohol (95 per cent.)

First dissolve the tartaric acid in a portion of the Arrack, and add it to the remainder. Next cut the oils in the alcohol, add this to the Arrack, and lastly add the syrup.

Essence of Roman Punch for Bottling.

> 1 quart of boiling Syrup.
> 1 quart of Brandy.
> 1 quart of Jamaica Rum.
> 21 Eggs.
> 1 Lemon.

Beat the eggs to a froth with the juice of the lemon; stir in the liquors; filter through felt or close flannel, and add the syrup. Bottle for use.

A little of this syrup in a tumbler two-thirds full of shaved ice, and well shaken, makes a delicious beverage.

Essence of Kirschwasser Punch for Bottling.

> 7 gallons of plain Syrup.
> 1½ gallons of Lemon Juice.
> 5 gallons of Kirschwasser.

Mix thoroughly and strain through canton flannel. Instead of lemon juice ½ pint of essence of lemon may be used.

Essence of Brandy Punch for Bottling.

> 5 gallons strong Brandy.
> 3 gallons plain Syrup.
> ½ pint of Tincture of Lemon peel.
> ½ pint of Tincture of Orange peel.
> 3 oz. Tincture of Allspice.
> ½ wine glass Tincture of Cloves.

Mix the tinctures with the brandy and add the syrup.

Root Beer.

> 1 oz. Yellow Dock.
> 1 oz. Wintergreen.
> 1 oz. Sassafras.
> 1 oz. Allspice.
> ½ oz. Coriander.
> ½ oz. Wild Cherry Bark.
> ¼ oz. Hops.
> 3 qts. Molasses.

Pour boiling water on the above and let stand twenty-four hours; strain and add half pint yeast. It will be ready in twenty-four hours.

Spruce Beer.

    2 oz. Hops.
    2 oz. Chips of the Sassafras Root.
    10 gallons water.
    Boil 20 minutes; strain and pour in while hot 1 gallon
        Molasses.
    2 table-spoons Essence of Spruce.
    2 table-spoons Essence of Ginger.
    1 table-spoon Essence of Ground Allspice.
Put it in a keg, and when cold add 1 quart yeast; after standing 24 hours draw it off or bottle it.

Wahoo Beer.

    2 oz. Sweet Fern.
    1 oz. Sarsaparilla.
    ½ oz. Wintergreen.
    1 oz. Sassafras.
    2 oz. Prince's Pine.
    2 oz. Comfrey Root.
    2 oz. Burdock Root.
    1 oz. Nettle.
    1 oz. Solomon's Seal.
    4 oz. Black Birch.
    4 oz. Raw Potatoes.
    4 gallons water.
Chop the potatoes up fine and boil all together 6 hours. Strain,
and add 1 quart molasses to 3 gallons of beer; brown a loaf of
bread and throw into the liquor; when almost cold, add 1 pint
yeast, let it ferment 1 day (24 hours) and bottle and bung it up
tight in a keg.

Plantation Beer.

    3 bunches Wintergreen.
    3 bunches Sarsaparilla.
    3 bunches Sassafras.
    3 bunches Sweet Fern.
    3 bunches Spicewood.
    3 bunches Prince Pine.
Grind together in a mill. Heat 8 gallons water. Put in ingredients while the water is hot. Boil one hour; strain, and
then boil ½ pound hops in three gallons water. Strain and
mix with the other, adding one gallon molasses. Brown a loaf
of bread; soak it in brewers' yeast. Put all together in a ten
gallon keg, let it ferment, and when done beat the white of an
egg to a froth. Stir thoroughly into the beer and bung the keg.
Let it stand until clear and bottle for use.

Molasses Beer.

Mix 4 quarts Molasses with 13 gallons water and 3 oz. Hops. Boil half an hour, strain and add ½ pint of Yeast.

Ginger Beer.

2 gallons water.
1 pint Molasses.
1 gill Yeast.
2 oz. ground Ginger.
This can be ready for use in two hours.

ANOTHER:

2 lbs. brown Sugar.
2 gallons boiling water.
1 quart Molasses.
2 oz. Cream Tartar.
2 oz. Ginger.
Stir well together. Put in a keg. Add a pint of good yeast; bung it up close. Shake the keg well, and after standing twenty-four hours bottle it, and in ten days it will sparkle like champagne.

Hop Beer.

5 quarts water.
6 oz. Hops.
Boil 6 hours, after which strain this, and adding 4 quarts more water and 12 table-spoonsful ground ginger, boil 3 hours longer. Strain this and mix with the former strained liquor. Deeply brown a loaf of bread, and pounding it fine add to the liquor, and when it is nearly cold add a pint of brewer's yeast, allowing it to ferment a day and a half (36 hours). Draw off into a keg or bottle ; tie corks down.

Lemon Beer.

1 gallon water.
1 Lemon sliced.
1 table-spoon ground Ginger.
1 pint Sugar House Syrup.
½ pint Yeast.
Mix thoroughly and let stand for one day (24 hours), when it will be ready to use. If bottled, tie down the corks.

Lager Beer.

This is of almost universal consumption, and much depends upon its handling. It should be kept at a temperature of from 40 to 45 degrees, and when the demand is sufficiently rapid is best drawn directly from the keg. Do not use the first two or three glasses, until the beer runs freely; then drive the vent into the bung. If drawn through pipes, they should be of the best material and kept perfectly clean and in good order. Beer remaining in the pipes over night should not be used, as it is liable to sicken whoever drinks it. The bartender must see that the glasses are perfectly clean. After filling, remove the superfluous froth with a ruler, as by this means the foam in the glass will remain firm lager, and prevent the beer from getting flat as quickly. If a second glass or more is called for, use the same glass, without rinsing. The beer will thus taste and look better. In serving two or more of a party, be careful not to mix the glasses, as that is unpleasant to the customers.

Bottled Lager must not be kept on ice, but in a very cool place in the ice box, in a standing position, to allow the sediment to settle.

Elderberry Beer.

Secure about twenty gallons of the first and strong wort.

Boil ½ bushel of elderberries and when cold strain them into the wort and let it work in the barrel. You will be surprised at the result. At the end of a year you will have an excellent Port wine.

Locomotive.—*(Use a large bar glass.)*

1 table-spoonful of genuine honey.
The yolk of a fresh raw Egg.
3 dashes of Curacoa.
1 claret-glass of red Burgundy.

Heat the wine in a thoroughly clean saucepan until it boils, then pour it gradually upon the other ingredients, (which, previously, should have been thoroughly beaten together in a mug or pitcher), whisking and stirring the materials all the while, in order to prevent the egg from curdling. Pour the mixture into a large bar-glass, powder a little cinnamon on top, and add two or three cloves before serving.

This seems like taking too much trouble just to make one glass of Locomotive. The following proportions of ingredients makes four nice glasses :

Take 2 ounces of honey.
2 poney-glasses of Curacoa.
1 quart of high red Burgundy.
A few drops of essence of Cloves.

Proceed as directed above, and serve in large goblets, previously heated.

Grape Wine.

Pick over carefully, thoroughly ripe grapes, free from stems and blemishes, press out the juice; to one quart of juice add one quart of water; (soft, boiled water is best,) add 1¼ pounds sugar. After it is done fermenting, bung up tight. It will be ready to draw off in 3 months or sooner, but will be a far better wine in a year, if left unmolested until then.

Parsnip Wine.

18 pounds of sweet Parsnips.
3 gallons of water.
Boil together soft, press liquor through a sieve, add to each gill 3 pounds of loaf sugar; when nearly cold add yeast. Let the wine stand open ten days, stirring from the bottom, several times each day.

Then put it in a cask, and keep it full up to the bung with liquor reserved for that purpose, as it works out.

Rhubarb Wine.

Chop the Rhubarb plant, drain off the juice, and to each quart add a quart of water and 2 pounds of sugar. Let it ferment, and bottle when clear.

Tomato Wine.

1 quart of Tomato Juice.
1 pound of Sugar.
Use no Yeast, as it will ferment without.
This is easy to make and is much relished in some places.

Blackberry Wine.

½ oz. ground Cinnamon.
¼ oz. ground Cloves.
1 drachm Cardamon Seeds.
1 drachm grated Nutmeg.
5 gallons Blackberries.
Mash the berries, pour on 5 gallons water, heat all to a boiling point, but do not let it boil. Add 1½ gallons white syrup; pour all into a 10 gallon keg, keep in a warm place, and the keg full. After fermenting, strain and press, add one gallon neutral spirits, filter and when clear, bottle.

Black Currant Wine.

5 gallons black Currants.
5 gallons water.
10 pounds crushed Sugar.

Dissolve sugar in the water. Heat all to 100 degrees Fahrenheit. Pour into a ten gallon keg, put in a warm place, keep it constantly full. After fermenting, strain and press, add one gallon spirits, 95 per cent. above proof, fine or filter and bottle when clear.

Ginger Wine.

3 gallons water.
3 pounds Sugar.
4 ounces Jamaica Ginger.

Boil one hour. Strain. Add 3 lemons chopped fine, and half a pint of yeast.

Mix together and pour into a keg. After it has fermented one week, draw it; it is ready for use.

Elderberry Wine.

8 gallons Elderberries.
12 gallons water.
60 lbs. brown Sugar.

Dissolve by boiling; add yeast and ferment. Add 4 pounds brandy, and bung it up for three months.

Gooseberry Wine.

7 lbs. brown Sugar.
40 lbs. Gooseberries.
Rain water to make 10 gallons.
1 quart Brandy.

Ferment.

Orange Wine.

23 lbs. Sugar.
10 gallons water; boil.

Clarify with the white of six eggs; pour the boiling liquid upon the parings of one hundred oranges, add the strained juice of these oranges, and yeast, six ounces; let it work for 3 or 4 days, then strain it into a barrel: bung it up loosely; in a month add 4 pounds of brandy, and in three months it will be fit to drink.

Birch Wine.

In February or March, bore holes in birch trees, and when you have secured 9 gallons juice, boil and skim, cooling it down to 100 degrees Fahrenheit. Dissolve in it 9 pounds sugar, adding two ounces lemon, cut fine; produce fermentation with 1 pint of gluten. Keep keg full constantly, when the fermenting is over, draw it off and strain, or filter into another keg in which you have burned a piece of brimstone paper.

Lemon Syrup for Soda Water.

Take 8 pounds of white sugar and 1 gallon of pure soft water, 2 ounces of gum arabic. Boil in a brass or copper kettle until the gum is thoroughly dissolved, then skim and strain through white flannel, adding tartaric acid, 5½ ounces, and flavor to taste with extract of lemon. Bottle.

All other syrups can be made in the same manner, using the extract of the fruit to taste. These make a very refreshing summer drink, by adding two table-spoonfuls of the syrup to a glass of water and ⅓ tea-spoonful of super-carbonate of soda; drink while foaming.

To Make Soda Water without a Machine.

In each gallon of water to be used, dissolve ½ pound of fine white sugar, and 1 ounce of super-carbonate of soda. Fill pint bottles with this mixture, have your corks ready. Now drop into each bottle ½ drachm of citric acid in crystals, and immediately cork and tie down. Handle the bottle carefully, and keep cool until needed.

Cherry Wine.

35 lbs. ripe Cherries.
5 lbs. brown Sugar.
Water to make eight gallons.
1½ pints best French Brandy.
Add Yeast, and set aside to ferment.

Red Currant Wine.

70 lbs. red currants, bruised and pressed.
10 lbs. brown Sugar.
Water to fill a fifteen gallon cask.
Ferment.
This makes a pleasant red wine, rather tart, but keeps well.